Dedication

To all of the wonderful dads who sent in their heartfelt contributions to this book. I admire the fact that you do not hesitate to be involved, care and advocate for your children. You all are amazing and your dedication is inspiring! The love that you have for your children and your families is a true testament to what it is to be a father. Your children are very blessed to have you in their lives.

Thank you for sharing your thoughts so freely and sincerely. This book would not have been possible without all of you and your willingness to share your experiences with an open heart and an open mind. I am honored that you trusted me with your heartfelt thoughts and am proud to be on this journey of autism awareness with you.

With love,
Judy

Acknowledgments

To Jennifer - Without all that you do for Jill (*and I*) these books would not be possible. Thank you for helping Jill to become the young woman that she is. You truly do have the magic touch with her, not only because of your expertise in the autism field, but because you have always believed in her and her abilities. I continue to be amazed at how confident and calm she can be because of all that you have taught her - such a wonderful gift you have given her. It means the world to me to know she is safe and happy in your care. Most of all, I am incredibly blessed and so thankful for how much you and your whole family love her. God bless you!

Thank you to all of my editors (*and friends*) who spent long hours on this book!
Bill, thank you for cutting into your family time to help me with editing, and arranging for me to meet William Christopher. You've been a good friend for a long time, bless you!
Gayle, my very best friend, thank you for taking the time to help with this book also. We have been through so much together, this is just one more thing, isn't it! Your arms are always open for me and you know how much I love you for that! *'I know people who love... ' to keep me sane!*
Yes!
and Diane, my sister, my friend – I can always count on your honest opinion, even when I am not ready for the truth! I love how you are so supportive and understanding of my life with Jill. Thank you for your encouragement and belief in 'our thoughts'!

Mike, thank you for the endless hours of listening to me plan... and procrastinate putting this book together. Most of all, thank you for always being there for me!

To Virginia, Jill's 'Gram' - the memories of your love and kindness are with us every day. You left this earth way too soon and yet I am eternally grateful to you for sharing your life with Jill and including her in your family. Even though Jill says that she knows you are in heaven, she still waits for you and looks forward to seeing you... and she always will. I know that God is holding you in His hands because certainly, you are what angles are made of.

As always, thank you Danny, for all of your help with every aspect of this wonderful book. Your positive outlook is always inspiring! Your belief in me is a great comfort and I am truly blessed to have you in my life – you forever have my heart.

Foreward

by Don King

It is hard for someone who does not have a child with autism to understand the impact it has on a family. It is one of the biggest challenges a parent could ever face. Like the contributors to this book, I also have a child with autism. And like many others, my son seemed to develop normally and then regressed, losing his interest in social interactions, verbal skills, and the ability to stay focused or make eye contact. My first reaction as he started to regress was similar to many initial reactions to a great loss: I was in denial. I thought, he's a boy; it's OK if he's behind verbally and socially. It was only after seeing him with other children his age that it really sank in. Something was obviously wrong. The emotional impact of recognizing that your child has autism is crushing, but going through that pain allowed me to move forward and become an advocate for my son's medical and educational needs.

In the same way, as a society we need to move past denial and recognize that the huge increase in autism is real. Autism has become a national emergency. With rates of 1 in 166 children being on the autism spectrum, it is affecting everyone. As parents, we know our children's behaviors could not have gone unnoticed or undiagnosed in the past. The more severe kids are not able to speak and most are unable to effectively communicate. Where are the 1 in 166 adults with autism? Something has changed, and we should be able to figure it out. Our society must make it a priority to find causes of and treatments for autism. In the mean time, we need public support for the intensive education that can make it possible for many of our children to become independent adults. Early intervention with behavioral therapies may be expensive now, but is a much better value for society when the alternative is an adult dependant on the system.

Through the individual stories in this book, of overcoming tremendous challenges with patience and love, we can better understand and empathize with what it means to be the parent of an autistic child. These fathers show how important it is to be involved. At a time when we may feel most pushed away from our family, we are most needed. In the face of incredible stress, we must be there. Supporting the rest of our family. Accepting and loving our children as they are, while always helping them do more.

For those of us who also have children with autism, these stories offer us hope and inspiration, and a sense of community through shared experience. This book reminds us that we are not alone, but part of something much bigger. We can come together to expand the strength of our community to advocate for our children.

In spite of all the adversity and pain, there is so much to celebrate. Our children have given us a new appreciation for even the smallest accomplishments. Less is taken for granted now, and more is appreciated. Patience, tolerance, and compassion are a part of our daily routine. With our children inspiring us we have the chance to make the world a better place.

Don King (father of Beau)
Hawaii Filmmaker
Co-Director of *Beautiful Son,* A documentary about healing autism
www.beautifulson.com

Introduction

The number of children diagnosed with autism, Aspergers, or Pervasive Development Disorder (PDD) has gone from 1 in 10,000 in the early 1990s to 1 in 166 as of this year, 2007. I have seen this number time and time again and still, it is shocking to me.

My oldest daughter, Jill, is 23-years-old and was diagnosed with autism at the age of 4½. Jill has come a long way over the years and yet still requires constant supervision. We have been through a lot together and I have always felt like no one really understood what our lives were like, and that has been frustrating for me. Surely, I thought there were other mothers feeling the same. So I came up with this book idea where moms from all over the world could share how they were really feeling about raising a child with autism, Aspergers or PDD. The response was incredible and resulted in *Autism: Heartfelt Thoughts from Mothers*, published in 2005.

While completing the mothers book I had many dads wanting "their turn" and so here I am with *Autism: Heartfelt Thoughts from Fathers!* All of the stories touched me deeply. As each story came, I knew I was doing the right thing by publishing all of the heartfelt thoughts of these dedicated parents. I am still amazed by everyone who trusted me with their most honest and sincere feelings... just because we share the special connection of having a child 'on the spectrum' as we now say (*referring to the autism spectrum which includes all levels of functioning*).

The fathers in this book have a lot to say, even those who only wrote a little bit. They show how their hearts are on their sleeves when it comes to their child or children with autism. Included are: fathers, step-fathers, a foster-father, and even a grandfather who is raising his grandson. Not only are these dads there for their children, they share how many of their dreams have been shattered and how they have had to reshuffle their priorities. These dads are so loving and yet stay strong when their family needs them. Many of them expressed being so supportive of their wives and mothers of their children, who are most of the time the primary care providers.

I asked for their thoughts regarding their Biggest Challenges, Greatest Blessings, and I asked them to offer some Words of Wisdom for other parents. Most followed this format but some wrote their own stories. One father's story is about their family's trip to a local retail store, one that we can all identify with. There are a couple of stories where the dad wrote about having to make the most difficult decision a parent can make — having to place their child in care outside of their own home. These stories, written so well and so honest, are ones that made my heart ache for there were many similarities to my own. I also had to face the fact that I could no longer care for my daughter alone. In a way it was a comfort to know that other parents know this pain. My hope is that others reading these stories will know what our lives are like and become more sympathetic to the decisions we are forced to make regarding our kids. If friends and family members who read this book come to realize what it is that we go through and that we need support and understanding from them, then perhaps the compassion they show our children will grow.

Also, I included photos of the fathers and their child (*or children*). So often we see the kids but not the fathers. As you will see, the photos make their stories come to life - real dads, real stories. These photos show the insurmountable love these fathers have for their children — a perfect example that a picture is worth a thousand words!

I did have one person say, "Why is a woman putting together a book for fathers?" I thought this was a great question. At first it seemed a natural sequence following the Mothers' book, but then I realized I had my own personal reasons for 'needing' this book. I was divorced from my daughter's father a couple of years before her autism diagnosis. When I started to receive stories from dads for this book, the heartfelt, honest, and vulnerable stories from dedicated dads; everything I knew that my daughter was missing, was validated. These stories became my lifeline and my motivation to continue making the effort to reconnect with him. These dads made me want to know, 'What was he thinking?' After years of our not speaking, we finally reconnected. Where his relationship goes from here with Jill, is something that I am at peace with and now can give to God. It is because of this book and the wonderful fathers who poured their hearts out that I am forever grateful, for they helped me open a door I otherwise may have left closed. They have given me new hope and faith. They have taught me to forgive – some more.

I hope all fathers who read these stories will find comfort in knowing they are not alone and know that they are so important in their children's lives. For mothers and wives, I hope that you know the fathers are dealing with autism (*just as we are*) the best they can and they *"also need a shoulder to lean on"* as Matthew said (*one of the fathers in the book, page 79*).

This is a book that you can give to friends, family, teachers and anyone to whom you want to understand you and life with your child. Find a story you identify with and make a connection with that father. Making their contact information available to all is an indication of their trust in the need to connect and be a resource for others.

These are some amazing Fathers!

With love and hope,
Judy Lynne

"Alone we can do so little
Together we can do so much"
- Helen Keller

To Ryan,
Bless you and Jennifer for
opening your heart, home,
and family to Jill
— for she would not be who she is
without you

♥

Table of Contents

Table of Contents

Special Father's Day

by Michelle M. Guppy

I was looking for a Father's Day card — among the dozens and dozens everywhere.
So many perfectly worded sentiments — for ordinary father's without a care.
"We'll pamper you dad!" - "You're the greatest!" - "Now lie down, relax, or play!"
"Do all the things that you love to do — on this your special day!"

"Yeah right, if only…" I chuckled. But for real dads — where are the cards for them?
The dad's whose sons have special needs; the dad's who have become extraordinary men.
The dad's who gave up fishing — and now only dream of a game of golf,
The dad's whose son's are in the hospital, because of pneumonia from a simple cough.

So many things about life they don't get — those ordinary dad's who have not a clue,
About what it's like to have a ten-year-old son, who cannot say, "Daddy, I love you."
About what it's like at the office, hearing others brag about their kids triple-play,
Knowing if he tried to talk to them, they would stare blankly and not know what to say.

So many kids choosing cards that proclaim, "Daddy, you're my hero!"
But what truly makes a hero, those little hands holding the card do not know.
That heroes are dad's who accept that their child, will not ever be a little-league champ,
Who instead cheer them on at therapy, while longing to take them to Boy Scout Camp.

Hero's are the men who day and night work hard, and yet find they are always broke.
Because of the expenses, equipment, & challenges, of a never-ending financial yoke.
They are the men who would give their life, for a treatment that would cure their son,
They are the men who understand the victory, in each tiny battle their child has won.

I give up and am too tired to keep looking, for that elusive 'Special Father's Day' card.
I have to laugh at the irony that this too — is something else that shouldn't be hard!
So instead I'll settle for writing on a piece of paper, "I love you with all of my might!"
From the son who understands that a hero,
                    is the daddy who cries as he prays every night.

— Happy "Special Father's Day" Todd —
and all "Special Father's" everywhere!

Bill & Jake

Ohio

Jake was diagnosed at 3 years

CONTACT:

billsnoeberger@clearwire.com

BIGGEST CHALLENGE(S)

My first reaction must have been, "What is autism?" I still remember the day when we heard that our beautiful son Jake was diagnosed in the autistic spectrum. I especially remember the look on Julie's (*my wife*) face. I could not tell if it was sadness, relief, anger or confusion!

All I did know that day is that we had our answers as to what was wrong with our son. Jake was born in October of 1997, two years after our beautiful daughter Stephanie. Jake was a beautiful baby. He slept well and was a fun 1-year-old. Jake was developing fine until sometime after he started drinking "cows milk." His condition worsened shortly after his MMR (*measles, mumps & rubella*) vaccine shot at 18 months. It was truly like Jeckle and Hyde. Our son began to digress in development, he began to throw tantrums and bang his head on the floor, he began to withdraw socially and when he began biting and scratching others we knew we had issues that we were uneducated about and unable to resolve at the time.

We were living in Seattle and I can still remember the times Julie spent crying (*she did not know I knew*) trying to figure out what was wrong with Jake. Pediatrician after pediatrician simply blew off the behavior and continued to prescribe antibiotic medicines and others. We even had his adenoids removed at the advice of one doctor. Finally, Julie asked me to move her out of Washington and back to Ohio, back to our network of family, friends and doctors we knew.

To our surprise very few people knew anything about our son and his diagnosis. Fewer were able to give us advice or direction on where to go. One doctor even told us we should prepare for the fact that Jake may have to be institutionalized. This was not an accepted answer to Julie; she started to research day and night, on the internet, by calling "so called" experts, and researching books, etc. Our own doctor, who was Jake's doctor at birth, could not see what was going on. I was in some sort of denial wondering how that could happen to my son, and at times, I would try to shut myself out from the issue. Not Julie. She persisted and changed my way of thinking when it came to traditional medicines and cures.

Slowly but surely Julie was becoming educated on the "Autistic Spectrum" which, quite honestly, is still extremely undefined to me! She began to load up on information about the MMR shot, about the diet, about hereditary enzymes and about the children within the Spectrum. Julie even became certified as a nutritionist.

We tried working with our pediatrician but that was not working initially. We finally zeroed in on a DAN (*Defeat Autism Now*) doctor in Ohio and went to see him. Several thousands of dollars later, my wife and I realized this was not a process to fix our son. This process at this particular practice seemed to deal with more adults and seemed to treat the symptoms instead of treating and attacking the cause. After numerous doctor visits, hundreds of trial fixes and thousands of dollars, we found Dr. Dave in Columbus, Ohio who started us on a path that I will never forget. Dr. Dave used homeopathic and biomedical procedures that seemed to make sense.

Dr. Dave listened to Julie and was aware of the issues children face today due to the lack of protection by our government from the profits of the pharmaceutical companies that rule our land. Dr. Dave tested Jake and found some of the causes in conjunction with Julie's research and findings. It would appear to me that one or two things that were bad created a domino effect in my son that took him away from us. The more we researched and tested Jake, the more we found was wrong with him. I can't tell you how lost and helpless I felt. I just wanted to numb myself from it and hope it would all go away.

Thank God my wife, Julie, put her foot down and drew her line in the sand! Julie began a regimen of testing and natural supplements. She began cooking meals all day that were gluten and dairy-free. Try pleasing a 5-year-old, a 3-year-old, and a 45-year-old husband with a diet like that! Amazingly though, there seemed to be a breakthrough! Not but a few days after taking certain enzymes and cutting out wheat and dairy, did Jake start to talk and communicate. We were still a long way off from normalcy but it was a milestone I will never forget. Jake actually spoke up and told Julie he was hungry. I truly had to go into a bathroom, as to not let Julie see my tears.

These supplements, special diets and homeopathic treatments would go on for years. The good news is, we were seeing small milestones and we were communicating a bit with Jake. Another piece of good news is that our daughter, Stephanie, who was 6-weeks premature was quickly developing into the upper bracket in every category in her age group. The bad news was the cost! None of this, regardless of the great results, was covered by insurance. It was all out-of-pocket and the debt was mounting. It was not that I cared, as I would spend each penny I earned to fix Jake, but the company I worked for had just gone chapter 7 and what was there, and a decent income one day, was literally gone the next along with my 401 and unpaid salary and expenses.

We made a decision to sell our home and a lot of our property. We were into heavy debt and could not keep up with the bills. Going Chapter 7 ourselves seemed to be a good option but Julie and I felt that would mean the '*spectrum*' would have beaten us. So we sold our beautiful home and moved into a much smaller rental home. We literally ate bologna sandwiches for most meals for a while, as what money we did have went to Jake's treatments, supplements and enzymes.

GREATEST BLESSING(S)

Through research, Julie found some assistance for Jake in a program called LLEP in Columbus. We enrolled Jake in this program and it broke my heart to see the number of children who qualified for this program and were considered to be in the '*spectrum*'. The personnel were amazing and we started to see some milestones we had not seen before. Little by little we were being rewarded for the tenacity of one woman who refused to give up on her son, Jake! Additionally, Julie introduced all of us to natural supplements and a better diet and to my surprise all of us have been much healthier.

I found great employment again and I was working very hard and doing a lot of business travel. I was handsomely rewarded for my efforts at work and this allowed Julie to get even more aggressive on her attack against the disease that had our son. We spent two years in that rental before we were able to build a modest new home in a great neighborhood. Dr. Dave and Julie continued to make progress with Jake and it soon became clear to Julie that she needed to take Jake's treatment to another level.

Eventually, we moved again to Dayton, Ohio and just as surprisingly Julie was able to find more people who were educated on the spectrum and were breaking ground with new supplements, techniques and treatments. Julie continued to volunteer as a State Rep for Unlocking Autism (*www.unlockingautism.org*) but quite honestly, had her hands full with our family, and people we knew and met who had children in the spectrum had enlisted Julie for help and advice. My hard work was being rewarded even more with a handsome income which allowed my wife to experiment with more treatments and, even more satisfying, she began to help others and provide the less fortunate with supplements and treatments.

Jake entering school was a scary proposition for us but luckily even the schools are becoming better equipped to work with these children as they continue to grow in mass. What used to be considered a discipline problem was becoming more recognized as chemical issues. Unfortunately the number of children put on prescription drugs also was growing at an alarming rate. Julie and I refused to go down this path.

Again, the cost was mounting and although at times hesitant, the results were proof so I continued to support Julie's decision to keep trying new and innovative ideas. Jake's first couple of years at school were a challenge but with the experience and knowledge my wife continued to gain, she was able to work with the educators and get Jake the proper intervention specialists. We were seeing milestones after Julie introduced specific enzymes to his diet and certain treatments and supplements seemed to add to his development.

Amazingly, Jake began to show progress in reading and even in simple math. This was truly astonishing to us and we began a regimented reading and homework discipline. Whatever happened to our son certainly did not affect our daughter as for 20 straight quarters in 1st through 5th grade she made the honor role and was noted at school to be especially caring and aware of special needs students.

After 2nd grade we knew we had accomplished amazing results but we were not honestly prepared for what was to happen in the summer between 2nd and 3rd grade. Julie had come across some additional supplements and treatments and almost as a miracle, our son began to process information and problems like we had never seen before. Jake knew there were issues with him and he was willing to forego things such as ice cream, sweets and deserts knowing that it would hurt him. We were able to find ice cream treats and other desert-type items he could eat such as "Rice Dream" frozen treats.

During this summer (2006) as we were preparing for 3rd grade, Jake continued to show amazing developmental progress, and a strong appetite. Julie was being sought out by groups all over the state to discuss her knowledge and treatments for Jake. Her story was published recently in a book called *That's Life with Autism: Tales And Tips for Families with Autism* by Donna Satterlee Ross and Kelly Ann Jolly, and she discussed these issues on WLW in November.

Jake is now in the 3rd grade and only has assistance on speech, to which he claims he wants to work his way out of. Jake has developed a big heartedness and a great sense of humor and can always be counted on for a good laugh. Jake is a better person at 8 than most people will ever be. My son has now started the 3rd grade and is in mainstream public schools in Ohio and has brought home 3 B's, 3 A's and a 100% on school papers. Jake is socializing, has a group of "best friends" and cannot determine if he likes Star Wars, Pokemon, or Avatar better! He even ribs me by cheering for Michigan to beat the Buckeyes.

Jake has become the glue of our family and Julie is a real life angel who refused to give in and has been fighting and winning now for 7 years. Our Stephanie is a typical 11-year-old girl who is into friends, music and loves school. She is extremely healthy and happy and like the rest of us, stays away from chemical enhanced foods and prescription drugs. I am lucky to be blessed with such a family and although I travel a lot and work long hours, not a day goes by I don't thank God for what I do have in our family. No possession, home, car or status symbol can compare to the pride of having our son back and better than ever!

WORDS OF WISDOM

My advice to other fathers is to reach out, give up your possessions, desires, and bring your children back from the clutches of this terrible spectrum. It can be done but you have to be ready for a fight. Support non-traditional measures and seek out support groups and others.

Boback & Arrian

Georgia

Arrian, age 9
Arrian was diagnosed at 3

BIGGEST CHALLENGE(S)

At the beginning, the biggest challenge was trying to understand my son. It is very frustrating for a nonverbal child to get his thoughts and feelings out. It was also a challenge to introduce him to society with limited communication skills. As he got older and more aware of his surroundings, challenges got more intense. Teaching an autistic child appropriate behavior in public and towards opposite sex during puberty can also be very challenging. The toughest challenge of all has been teaching others about autism and autistic individuals.

"The toughest challenge of all has been teaching others about autism"

GREATEST BLESSING(S)

Arrian is the greatest blessing in my life. Not only is he sweet, understanding, and loving towards us, he is really great with others. All of the above challenges and problems go away with his handsome little grin and an " I love you" in sign language. One of his greatest characteristics is that the sincerity, love and respect never fade away with age. It makes me want to reevaluate the terms "normal and abnormal."

WORDS OF WISDOM

Until the day that we can unlock this complicated puzzle, there are three magical words: **Love**, **Patience** and **Persistence**, which can cure most any condition.

"Love, patience and persistence can cure most any condition"

B & T

Florida

BIGGEST CHALLENGE(S)

My biggest challenge is getting "T" away from the video games. He is obsessed with anything video: gameboys, video games, even the television. I believe he would starve to death if we didn't turn off the television.

GREATEST BLESSING(S)

I expected the kids at school to pick on him but instead most have watched over him and helped him in school. Maybe they have learned something about themselves along the way. I know I have.

WORDS OF WISDOM

It took a long time for me to accept the fact that this is a disability. It would be easier to accept his behavior if he was in a wheelchair or blind or something like that. I am finally accepting the fact that some things will never change but life still goes on.

We became foster parents a couple of years after our youngest son was killed. Maybe we thought more kids could fill the void he left. They don't. But they do keep us busy and that is what we need. Falling in love with them was a bonus.

Brian & Brian

Colorado

Brian, age 3

BIGGEST CHALLENGE(S)

The biggest challenge is trying to communicate with my son, Brian. He is 32-months-old and non-verbal. His receptive and expressive language is less than that of a one-year-old. We are currently working on sign language and PECS (*Picture Exchange Communication System*). It is almost like going to another country without knowing the language but still being expected to understand the people. It would be incredibly frustrating to try to get our needs met. I feel bad that Brian can't tell us what he wants. With sign language or two-word sentences, Brian could get his point across. By telling us what food(s) he feels like eating, for example, it would help incredibly in his nourishment. It is a huge struggle to get him to eat a simple meal because he is a very picky eater.

I feel like people do not understand autism and that is a challenge. Everyone thinks autism means you are a genius or insane. They don't understand it is a disability like Down Syndrome or Cerebral Palsy and it affects everyone differently.

GREATEST BLESSING(S)

His greatest blessing is his innocence. He thinks of hurting no one. Nor, has he the slightest intention of cheating, stealing or destroying anything or anyone. He is a happy boy most of the time. Every day, I get to see the perfect innocent angel God gave me.

WORDS OF WISDOM

The only words of wisdom I can think of are patience and understanding. Brian can be charming and a lot of fun to be around. To really help him through his rough times and effectively guide him on a daily basis, it is of the utmost importance to fully understand his needs and behaviors. It's critical to exercise patience as well as understanding.

Try to find other dads with kiddos with special needs. I feel they can relate more to me and my struggles.

FAVORITE RESOURCES

Books:
Facing Autism by Lynn M. Hamilton
The Out of Sync Child by Carol Stock Kranowitz and Lucy Jane Miller
The Out of Sync Child has Fun by Carol Stock Kranowitz and T.J. Wylie
Unraveling the Mysteries of Autism and PDD by Karyn Seroussi

Websites:
Autism Society of America - www.autism-society.org
The Autism Research Institute

Whoever does not LOVE
does not know GOD,
because GOD is LOVE.
~1 John 4:8

Brian & Nathan

Idaho

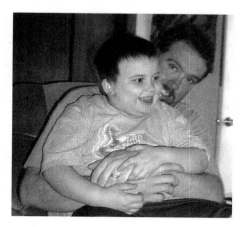

Nathan, age 6
Nathan was diagnosed at 2

CONTACT:
brianf66@msn.com

BIGGEST CHALLENGE(S)

Our son was born November 18, 1998. He was our first child and the joy of our life. Everything seemed normal at first but when he stopped talking, and seemed to be regressing, we started seeking answers. The hardest part was putting a 2-year-old through a battery of tests ranging from a sleep hearing test with electrodes glued to his head, to a CAT scan. Watching your child go through all of this, with this 'why are you doing this to me' look in his eyes, is heart-wrenching. Fortunately, we did push for answers and received a diagnosis at an early age. We began an early intervention program to give him all of the help he needed to succeed. Nathan has made miraculous progress thanks to my wife's push for everything he needs.

GREATEST BLESSING(S)

Nathan is a joy to have as a son! While he does have his challenges in life, he is always cheerful and brings a smile to everyone's face. He loves his movies and will do anything for a movie reward. His favorite thing in the world is to crawl into bed with me and my wife and get snuggle time. He pulls us both together saying, "my mommy, my daddy" and makes the world great. His smile is always infectious and has made his teachers and teachers' aides willing to go that extra mile just to help him. While he does have his moments and is a challenge, when he looks at me with his big eyes and says, " Daddy, you are my best friend," everything else just doesn't matter.

WORDS OF WISDOM

Pay attention as your child grows up and if something doesn't seem right then search for reasons why because, as with most things in life, early intervention makes all the difference. While having an autistic child can be a challenge and a stress in both your family and professional life, the rewards of seeing him or her overcome and achieve make it all worthwhile. Don't let other people, whether they are friends, teachers, or family tell you what is best for you child. You are the parent and are in the best position to know what is best. Don't shut yourself off, take it all in and in the end make your own choices for what is best for you and your child. Also, do not forget your other children. Do not let your autistic child become so central to your world that you make them feel second place. Include them in activities and as the other children get older explain to them about autism so they understand why their brother or sister needs a little extra help. Most of all, love your child and support them.

Bruce & Peyton

Arkansas

Peyton was diagnosed with
Aspergers at 5 years

CONTACT:

marycogburn@sbcglobal.net

BIGGEST CHALLENGE(S)

There are many challenges in being Peyton's father. The biggest are communication and keeping up with him. Sometimes it is so hard to understand the point he is trying to get across. He is like the Energizer Bunny: he just keeps going and going...

GREATEST BLESSING(S)

There are so many blessings and the greatest has to be Peyton's personality. He is so wonderful, with a unique personality. Another incredible blessing has come from the way our church family has opened their arms and so willingly accepted Peyton with his disability.

WORDS OF WISDOM

I have one major word of wisdom to all the fathers out there going through the same problems and at the same time:

Be patient through all the rough times and be thankful for all the great times.

"Be patient through all the
rough times and be thankful for all
the great times"

Dan & Alena

Tennessee

Alena was diagnosed with
Aspergers at 8 years

CONTACT:

Dgd3420@hughes.net
615/319-0460

BIGGEST CHALLENGE(S)

Cheryl, my wife, and I were married in 1991 and our first child, Alena, was born three years later. We knew from the start that there was something special about Alena. She just didn't respond to us like we have seen other babies respond to their parents. We moved to Nashville, Tennessee in 1997 and soon after had her tested, the diagnosis was PDD-NOS, (*Pervasive Development Disorder-Not Otherwise Specified*). We had heard of autism but didn't really know what it was, let alone PDD-NOS and so began our journey. We began weekly therapy sessions at Bill Wilkerson Center of Vanderbilt University Hospital for speech and language plus minimal services that we were getting through the school system.

When Alena started kindergarten her services through the public schools stayed pretty much the same but added a kindergarten inclusion teacher (*this person was supposed to make her transition into kindergarten smoother*). Well, this person wanted to move her into a special education class because she had autism. She didn't take into consideration Alena and HER individual needs, she just used a blanket statement on autism and took it upon herself to make the changes on her own without consulting with Cheryl or I.

Kindergarten finished up with as little drama as we could take, i.e., 3 to 4 hour M-team meetings. It finished up better than it started only from the wonderful and understanding teacher that Alena had. Alena loved going to school and responded well to her teacher. Then first grade came along and we were presented with a new challenge. We had a teacher that was not as understanding and helpful as the kindergarten teacher was; she did her job as required but gave us no help with Alena.

Second grade was absolutely wonderful for Alena. She had a teacher that worked with us and wanted to give Alena the best chance she could give her. Third grade started the same way that first grade had. After the first semester, Cheryl and I decided that I should come off of the road traveling (*I'm a musician*) and home-school Alena. This was the best move that we could have made for her. It's been three years now that I have been home-schooling her and she is developing faster that anyone could have imagined.

For Alena our biggest challenge was trying to get her to understand if we varied from a plan. We would tell her that we would go out to eat then go shopping then to the grocery store. If Cheryl and I changed our mind and went shopping first she would have a total meltdown. After several years of having a plan before we left the house she finally understands that it's not the end of the world if we don't do things in a certain order.

GREATEST BLESSING(S)

The greatest blessing that Alena has given me is the fact that she is my daughter. She has a wonderful sense of humor and a very compassionate heart. She has really taught me the true meaning of patience and understanding.

FAVORITE RESOURCES

Autism Society of Middle Tennessee - www.autismmidtenn.org
Tony Attwood - www.tonyattwood.com.au
Home Schooling Special Needs Children - www.nathhan.com

Darren & Jacob

Arizona

Jacob, age 7
Jacob was diagnosed at 5 years old

CONTACT:
Montello1@juno.com

BIGGEST CHALLENGE(S)

Having a son with special needs has really challenged me as a dad. It has caused me to think about different things I never had to when raising my first two sons. I have had to make a lot of changes in my expectations. I have had to take a different road. I try to focus on what he can do and try to overlook what he can't do. I have had to be a lot more patient and more understanding. It has made me much more of a compassionate father. My adjustment to less sleep at night has been a challenge for me. Jacob is my alarm clock, as he doesn't seem to require as much sleep, as a typical child would need. Once he is up, he makes sure I am up. He often wanders around the house at night and that, in itself, presents many challenges. I certainly am much more alert to listening for him at night and I have adjusted to it. At times it can be discouraging when trying to explain to others why my son has special needs. Not everyone has enough patience for him and that can be a very disappointing.

GREATEST BLESSING(S)

I think the greatest blessing I experience with Jacob is his love that he shares with me. He likes to follow me around and enjoys being my little helper.

Jacob makes me feel good when he wants to learn something. I feel blessed to be able to be there to coach him thru his struggles in life. I love to eat lunch with him at school whenever I get a chance. When he sees me and smiles, his whole face lights up and he makes me feel proud to be his dad. He feels really safe with me. I believe he feels I understand him and his challenges. I have become his greatest fan when watching him try baseball or soccer. It's not about the competition of who's winning or not winning the game, just that he is having fun and we are having fun together. It is such a blessing to see him smile when he accomplishes something.

> "It [autism] has made me much
> more of a compassionate father"

WORDS OF WISDOM

When a father learns about any difficulty or problem in their child's development, this information comes as a tremendous blow. One of the first reactions is that of denial – 'This cannot be happening to me, to my child, to our family.' You cannot change the fact that your child has a disability, but you can make a tremendous contribution to your child's life by being the best father you can be. Many things can be done to help you through this period of trauma. Be assured that there are programs available to help you out, there will be progress in your child, and there will be help of many kinds and from many sources. Make sure you take time out to do things you enjoy.

Make sure if you are married to spend time with your wife. Most of the time the caregiving tends to be the mom. Driving back and forth with therapies and doctor appointments will put a strain on your wife. It is important to be a part of planning your child's education. Go to the IEP (*Individualized Education Program*) meetings anytime you get a chance. Be a part of the process of getting all the help you can and work as a team with your wife. Also make sure, if you have other children, that you plan things to do with them alone. Dad-time alone with each child makes a big difference. Understand that you don't have to have all the answers when parenting a child with special needs. Rejoice in all of his accomplishments – great or small. Accept that it is okay to feel discouraged every now and then.

20

David & Mandy

New Mexico

Mandy, age 23
Mandy was diagnosed at 11

CONTACT:

www.MandysFarm.org

BIGGEST CHALLENGE(S)

The biggest challenge raising a daughter with autism was striking the balance between giving her what she needed without allowing our son to become a second class sibling because he was normal (*gifted actually*). We managed to raise our daughter without ever becoming a dysfunctional family, and she has a sibling who adores her and will always be there for her in the future.

Another great challenge was deciding how to manage for her long-term care. Not wanting to leave New Mexico, and not finding any suitable living situation, prompted us to build Mandy's Special Farm (www.mandysfarm.org) in rural Albuquerque where Mandy and 5 other young women with autism can have fulfilling lives. The project was enormous, but with wonderful support from family and friends, it is a reality.

GREATEST BLESSING(S)

The greatest blessing was suddenly coming to the realization that some things simply cannot be fixed and need to be accepted with grace, humility, and humor. Mandy, our 23-year-old daughter with autism, is probably the happiest and most genuine person I know. I am blessed by the simple joy she always finds in dogs, hummingbirds, oscillating lawn sprinklers and French fries from McDonalds. Her life is simple and good and she has taught me to see the beauty in it.

"Love them for who they are"

WORDS OF WISDOM

Don't stop trying to maximize your child's abilities, but don't make them miserable trying to fix them. Love them for who they are.

David & Ben

Illinois

Ben, age 4
Ben was diagnosed at almost 2 years

CONTACT:
davidroyko@yahoo.com
Website:
www.geocities.com/davidroyko/mypage

A NEW LIFE

In our pre-autism days, before the boys turned two, we took them to a kids' concert. When the music began blasting from the stage, Ben and his twin brother Jake, who had been happily toddling through the aisles, each bolted for a parent. Karen scooped up Jake, and as soon as I picked up Ben, he pressed himself into my shoulder like a cuddly refrigerator magnet, my hand on his back, his hands grasping me tightly in terror. Before the second song ended, Jake was back on the ground, but Ben had not budged, his face burrowed into the warm, soft spot where my neck meets my shoulder. When the third song ended, I pulled Ben back a bit, to see if he still seemed scared. That's how I learned about one of Ben's defenses: if the situation is too much to take, if he feels overwhelmed, it's lights out. And in the face of this sonic onslaught, Ben had fallen sound asleep.

Nearly a dozen years later, this memory rushed in as Jeromi, Ben's Unit Supervisor, told us that Ben had fallen asleep early, before eight o'clock, on this, the first night of his "new life" at the Developmental Training Center (DTC).

The weekend before Ben's move had been, amazingly, one of the best we can remember. Amazing, because the previous three months – since the meeting where the school district had agreed with us that Ben needed a residential educational program – seemed to bring daily reminders of why Ben needed to go to the DTC. If we were religious folks, we'd be saying that God was helping us accept our decision by making life with Ben's autism more impossible by the day. (*If we were religious folks, we would have asked, long ago, why Ben had to be autistic in the first place.*) His non-compliance – regarding toileting and other behaviors – was becoming routine with everyone but Daddy, the only member of Ben's circle bigger, and stronger, than Ben, and Ben seemed to know it.

At the same time, the days and weeks leading up to Ben's move had a surreal quality to them, swinging from, "We can't make it another day with Ben at home," to, "We can't bear the thought of sending him away." Even though Ben's autism seemed determined to help us accept our decision, emotionally, it felt a bit like we were ticking off the days to an execution. When he was being "difficult," it was helpful to have a firm date approaching when his autism would be managed and treated by someone else. But, especially when Ben was happy, I always felt a huge wave of guilt for what was coming, for what was going to happen to him, for what he would soon be going through.

Karen was busy during Ben's last weekend at home, getting his stuff ready (*and there was A LOT of stuff*) for the move, so Ben had almost uninterrupted "Daddy time" Saturday, Sunday and Monday. The high points of the weekend were a couple of nice, long family swims that we took in Round Lake, courtesy of a good friend (*and Ben's lawyer*) who lives on the lake. Round Lake is extremely shallow, so we could spend hours in water that never goes above my waist. Ben was so happy and relaxed, and interactive, that we decided Round Lake is his single favorite place in the world.

The low point of the weekend, for me anyway, was breaking the news to Ben about his impending move. We did this Sunday morning with a "social story," something we use to help explain major events or plans to Ben. It takes the form of a short book of 8x10 sheets with simple sentences (*one per page*) and pictures, laminated and bound with three metal rings (*in other words, durable!*).

The "cover" says "Ben Royko and the DTC."

Page 1: On Tuesday, Ben will go to a New School! [Picture of the front door of the DTC.]
Page 2: The School is called the D-T-C. [Another picture of the front door of the DTC.]
Page 3: The DTC is in Wisconsin. [Blank map of Wisconsin with a red dot where it is, and below that, a photo of the "Wisconsin Welcomes You" sign you see at the border, which Ben recognizes from the many long drives we've taken.]
Page 4: Ben will have New Teachers at the DTC, like [photo] Jeromi, and [photo] Eric, [etc.]
Page 5: Ben will make New Friends with the Children at the DTC! [Pics of groups of kids.]
Page 6: Ben will Sleep Over at the DTC. [Pic of dorm room.]
Page 7: Mommy and Daddy Will Visit Ben at the DTC! (A photo of Mom, Dad, Jake and Ben having fun on a water ride.]
Page 8: Ben will Have Fun at the DTC! [fun pics]

As soon as Ben finished the story, he had his only cranky stretch of the weekend. Coincidence, maybe, but I truly think he "got it." For me, it felt like I had just done the most awful thing I had ever done to anybody in my life. I could not imagine what it must be like to be a kid like Ben, who hates transitions; who has virtually never spent a night away from Mom or Dad; who fears change and new things; who loves his Mom and Dad like all kids do; who, developmentally, is in many ways still very much a young child (*regardless of being, at 12, over 6 feet and 250 pounds*) and then to be told that you are going to be left at a new strange place, while being unable to (*verbally*) express your feelings about all of this, or even to ask a question. I found myself standing in the kitchen, away from Ben so I wouldn't increase his angst, unable to verbally express my own feelings as I sobbed.

The rest of the day was fun, with the trip to the lake and then a Father's Day gathering at Karen's parents' house, where Ben's aunts, uncles and cousins each told him they would come and visit him at his wonderful new school.

I can only assume that Ben applied some good old fashioned denial to his situation, because, except for immediately after reading his social story, he remained chipper right through the drive up to the DTC. When we got there, he complained about going in, which is typical for Ben and unfamiliar places (*though he had visited the place with us a month or so ago*). Once in the door, he was not interested in meeting anyone, and seemed slightly agitated. We made a quick trip into the bathroom, where he told me, clearly and emphatically, "Go to the car." I had to tell him, "No Ben, we're staying here."

The next stop was the infirmary with the nurse, and Ben was not in the mood to be examined. We said good-bye to Ben (*the "little" good-bye — the "big" good-bye would come later*) as Karen and I went to meet with the various people who would be working with Ben. It was a strange feeling to leave an unhappy Ben with strangers. The urge to swoop in and try to calm him down and protect others from any potential behavioral shrapnel was hard to resist but, at the same time, offered a tiny taste of the unfamiliar freedom we would soon experience.

Our meeting with the staff lasted for more than two hours. As has been the case with every contact we've had with the people at the DTC thus far, we felt like Ben was going to the right place. The people seem very competent, compassionate, sensitive, understanding, bright, experienced, and just plain nice. They also seem to truly "get" Ben and his needs. Ben's life will be structured with programming 24/7. From the moment he opens his eyes in the morning through bedtime, he will be busy. Even his "down time" is scheduled. This is what Ben needs, and it is also what he likes. Ben loves to be busy, and he enjoys finishing tasks. It really seems that the DTC will get Ben to reach his potential, which he can't do any longer at home. The fact that we are confident of the quality of the people and the DTC in general is what has allowed us to do this, the almost-unthinkable.

More difficult to grasp is going a month before our first visit with him. The staff feel, and we agree, that Ben should be settled in before our first visit, so that when he has to separate from us, even if it is a hard separation, he will be in a place that he knows, feels safe and comfortable in, and likes. However, it is incredibly hard to imagine, especially for Karen, who has rarely been apart from Ben since birth – no, make that gestation – going an entire month without seeing him, hugging him, kissing his soft, chubby little cheeks, and seeing his sweet, beaming smile.

After the meeting, we unloaded his stuff and went up to his unit (*or "pod," sort of a cross between the floor of a dormitory and an in-patient psych ward, but brighter*) to see him one last time before saying good-bye. As we entered his pod, I had an all-too-familiar Ben experience — I could hear him before I could see him. Ben was yelping and crying as he came into view, standing just outside his bedroom. As soon as he saw us, he made it clear he wanted all of us to leave. The week before, Karen had expressed the hope that we'd be able to help him unpack and settle into his room before we left, but that was her eternal optimism talking. In the reality of the moment, Ben was freaking out, and as long as we stayed, that wouldn't change. It was time to say good-bye.

It was quick, a long good-bye would only make things harder. I gave Ben a big bear hug, said "I'll see you soon!" and headed out the door as Karen said her farewell, which I couldn't watch. Very briskly we walked down the hall and out of the door, accompanied by the sound of Ben's wailing.

To describe the week since as an emotional roller coaster only hints at the experience. It is heartbreaking to imagine Ben being heartbroken. What is he thinking? Does he know he will see us again? That we still love him? Autism's hallmark of being unable to conceive of other people's subjective inner life means he probably can't really wonder if we still love him (*or that we "love" at all – autism gives new meaning to that age-old poet's question, "What is love, anyway?"*), but he certainly can wonder why the people he loves most in the world, that he has always known and relied upon and trusted, have abandoned him.

As we have always strived to differentiate between Ben and autism, we do not miss the autism for all of the shit (*figuratively and very literally*) that it has forced upon all of us, but as for Ben, we miss him so much it feels like our guts are being ripped out of us.

At the same time, the change for the remaining three of us in our household has been profound. I knew it would be very different, but after so many years of gradually adjusting everything in life to accommodate autism, it was only when it was gone did I come to understand the extent that it had become — had to become — the core of our daily lives. Removing autism from our lives was like having the framework, the entire skeletal structure of our lives ripped out, leaving an immense, gaping void that now required us to rebuild the framework of our household. We have been living in a house that has had to be more and more "baby-proofed" as Ben's size and strength grew far beyond his developmental age. We were sitting on couches and chairs that had been broken and pulverized, replacement promising only more destruction. We could never let Ben out of our sight, so someone always had to be on "Ben duty." Going out meant either leaving one parent with all of the burden, or paying much more than typical sitter wages to one of the very few who could handle Ben while we waited for the cell phone to ring with a crisis. Autism meant unpredictable bed times, unpredictable nights, and unpredictable wake-ups. Going places with Ben had become virtually impossible accept for a few standard outings to therapists and the like. At any moment, anywhere, anytime, there was a good chance Ben's bowels or bladder would bring about the kind of event that most parents recount for the rest of their lives as their big parenting horror story, but for us was business as usual. These and a thousand other aspects big and small were now history, or at least someone else's problem to solve. Ben is where those issues actually can be solved through 24-hour a day behavioral programming that should eventually re-hardwire his brain through behavioral repetition.

That evening, Jake had a couple of friends sleep over, which was good because it kept him from hearing the heavy silence and feeling the uncanny calm of the house that first night. At about 9:30, Karen and I, anticipating the stampede to the kitchen looking for a snack, called up to the boys, "Let's go get some ice cream." We grabbed the dog, crowded into the van, headed to Baskin Robbins, and ate our ice cream on the bench outside the store. For Jake, it was a first: He had never had the experience of a spontaneous trip with Mom and Dad, and friends, to get ice cream. It was our first "normal" experience as a family, the kind of normalcy that most people take for granted, but for us, it was anything but normal. It was extraordinary.

This will be Jake's first summer where his parents can take him places and do the things that make summer, and if it were happening any later, it might have been too late. We're catching him at the tale end of his childhood before his hormones command that he totally hate and never come near us, and we're going to try to make the most of it.

We have called the DTC every evening, and the reports have been good with the exception of eating. You will not use up both hands when counting the foods Ben will eat, but the staff was committed to getting Ben to try other foods besides grilled cheese and plain hot dogs. Besides a couple of snacks and the plain yogurt and the apple juice that are mixed with his medications, Ben ate very little in his first few days, refusing the offerings at meals, though he was able to sit as others ate, which is a stretch for Ben, as the sight of others eating can make him sick. Then Sunday, a breakthrough! Ben ate Sugar Frosted Flakes for breakfast, a corndog for lunch after the coating had been stripped (*a hot dog, yes, but very "different" from what he was used to*), and for dinner, he removed the ham from his ham and cheese sandwich and ate the cheese sandwich, again a combination of old (*cheese and bread*) and new (*"raw"*). He also tried and then ate Jell-O! He's on his way.

On his seventh day at the DTC, Karen and I had a telephone "conversation" with Ben. Ben's not a phone person. He listens for a moment but soon pushes away the receiver, which is why Ben was brought to an office with a speakerphone for the call, our first contact with him since his move. From our side, we sang him a favorite song, recited some of his favorite phrases (*"Go Clifford, go!"*) and, among other things, told him how much we love him. Ben said, "The piggy says oink!" By Ben standards, it was a wonderful phone call, and we felt good about it.

So far, we've heard that his behavior has been good, with few outbursts, and no out-and-out tantrums beyond the first few hours after we'd left. His mood sounds like it is improving, and my daily question of "Did he smile at all today?" is bringing more affirmative answers. Though we won't be seeing him for a few more weeks, we've arranged, with the staff's OK, some visits by friends and extended family for the interim, beginning this weekend, which we expect him to enjoy. Karen and I are counting the days until we get to see our little Benny boy.

So, after one week, it sounds like Ben is rising to the occasion in grand fashion. As for us, we are adjusting to the most immense change we have ever experienced, second only to having Jake and Ben in the first place, almost 13 years ago. Jake, after expressing some strong feelings of missing Ben, also said, "I've never felt this relaxed before." Until now, we hadn't really realized how autism and its constant requirements had made us so physically tense, every minute. After the second night of our new life, Karen said, "It feels like I've taken a muscle relaxant."

If it only had been that simple.   (June 27, 2006)

> "The other day, someone asked us if we'd gotten used to this new life yet, and I said, 'No, and I hope we never do' "

Ben update
(July 27, 2006)

I don't know if this is just a sort of honeymoon period, but Ben's transition has gone amazingly well so far. It's been over a month now, and virtually all the reports have been glowing. He's now had five visits from his favorite people: Karen's sister and her husband; then Pam, who has been working with Ben since he was 3; Karen's parents; Karen's brother Jordy; the Big Visit – us; and Karen with Ben's brother Jake. I really think the visits that took place before Karen and I visited – which all went wonderfully – established the pattern that people come, visit, and leave, which made the "farewell" after our visit go smoothly. In fact, when we stood up to leave, Ben bolted up with us, saying "car." We said, "No Ben, your going to stay here with Chad (*his teacher*), but we'll be back soon for another visit!" Then we hugged him and, as we turned to go, Ben hugged Chad. We can't be sure, but it seemed that Ben was able to comfort himself by hugging Chad as we left, which says plenty regarding his comfort level and the sense of security he's developing with the people at the DTC. It was a moment as encouraging as it was poignant, if not also a touch heartbreaking.

28

He's continuing his life-long growth spurt (*he's now 6'3"*), and between that and his new eating regimen (*the other day, he actually ate scrambled eggs*), he is slimming down nicely. From what we can tell, he's thriving in the wall-to-wall programming. Every report and every visit provides us with more assurances that he's precisely where he needs to be.

As for Karen and I, we miss Ben every day, sometimes achingly so, but at the same time, every day without the tsunami of autism saturating the life of our family feels like a vacation. That Ben is doing well allows us to truly enjoy our new life. If anything good has come from life with autism, it is a profound appreciation for the every-day — a sense of the ordinary feeling extraordinary. Even having a cold for the past week has been almost enjoyable because now, a cold is just a cold, not a reason for panic (*Ben gets cold, gets cranky, won't eat or drink the stuff with his meds, sleep goes completely wacky, behavior spirals out of control, etcetera, et-freaking-cetera*).

The other day, someone asked us if we'd gotten used to this new life yet, and I said, "No, and I hope we never do."

Derek & Noah

Wyoming

Noah was diagnosed at almost 3 years

Biggest Challenge(s)

My wife and I have been married 21 years as of 2006 and have a 7-year-old son, Noah, who was diagnosed with autism when he was almost 3. We also have a 19-year-old daughter who is away in college now.

One of the biggest challenges in raising Noah is that he can't tell me how he feels either emotionally or physically. When he's sad or scared, I just have to guess based on his behavior, and it's not always easy to tell. If he's sick he can't tell me "My throat hurts" or "I feel like throwing up". We have to monitor him very carefully for illness since he won't tell us if he feels any symptoms. He can talk about the things he sees and hears around him, but not about how he feels in his mind or body. He can talk pretty well as long as he's labeling things or identifying people, but he has no idea how to communicate feelings or physical discomfort and pain. It's disconcerting as a parent not to know when he's feeling sick or why he's frustrated and angry in a certain situation. It makes helping him much more difficult.

It's also hard knowing that his life is going to be totally different than what I thought the day he was born. All my dreams had to be tossed out and new ones found. It's not easy to find new dreams for his future when you really have no idea how the autism will affect his life in the long run. My wife felt her feelings about our son having autism immediately but mine were a long time in coming to the surface. For a while I thought he would eventually "get better" and his autism would just fade away. Now I realize that it is a life long thing that will affect every aspect of his life – and ours.

Another challenge is learning to get into his world when he can't get into mine. His mind naturally works differently than mine, even though his core feelings are the same ones I have. The ways he uses to achieve those feelings are just different than the ways I use. Even though it's sometimes hard for me to understand what he's thinking or why he enjoys a certain activity, I have to realize it's even harder for him to understand the way my mind works. After all, I have dozens of books I can read about autism, but he doesn't have a single book to help him understand us neuro-typicals! Since I have more capacity to be flexible than he does it becomes my responsibility to join him in enjoying many of the things he likes. Of course there are times when I need to help him enter into other more unfamiliar worlds that he will need to be familiar with in order to get along when he's older. Those times can be difficult, but he's a trooper and he puts up with it... most of the time.

I guess the last challenge I should write about is the subject of introducing him to God. How do I explain the existence of a purely spiritual being to a boy who, due to the structure of his brain, struggles mightily with comprehending anything he can't see, hear, feel, taste or touch? I'm stumped, but I still talk to him about God even though I don't know how much of the concept he can grasp. Perhaps as Noah grows older this subject will be easier for him to understand.

GREATEST BLESSING(S)

Without a doubt, I believe the greatest blessing in Noah is the fact that he is absolutely without guile. Because of his autism he is virtually incapable of telling a lie or manipulation. Deceit is just not a concept that enters his mind. If he wants someone to leave, he says so. If he wants something he shouldn't have, he says so. It's an odd silver lining in the cloud of autism, but I'm glad that when he IS able to communicate effectively it's with complete honesty. I always know that if he tells me something he's telling the truth every time. For instance, if he says he hears a lawn mower or an ambulance siren and nobody else can hear it, I know he really hears it. Not only is his hearing keener than mine but he just doesn't make things up. He doesn't see any point in making things up – it's just not practical to his way of thinking.

He also has a great sense of humor. This boy is funny, I mean, he's really entertains himself at times by doing silly things. He comes up with his own jokes and just howls with laughter sometimes! He loves to bring others in on the joke, and the sound of Noah laughing is like the sun bursting through the clouds on an overcast day.

We're also very fortunate that he is physically affectionate. He doesn't always know how to show it in appropriate ways, but I'm grateful for any display of love from him, from kisses to hugs to his peculiar way of rubbing the necks of people he really likes. I'm also glad that I can laugh or get excited with him when he "stims" over something that excites or pleases him. I used to cringe a little when he did that, especially when we were in public. Now I see it as his way of expressing his pleasure. Noah is not an embarrassment to me anymore. I'm proud of him. I'm proud of the progress he makes whenever he learns a new word or concept. He's my boy.

WORDS OF WISDOM

Children with autism are just like you and me inside. They perceive the world differently than we do and react to it differently, but inside they all have the same basic emotions of happiness, sadness, desire, etc. Most of all, they have the same need to be loved that we all have. Someone told me once, "Don't look at your child as an autistic person. Instead look at them as a person who happens to have autism." Autism isn't their identity. They are human just like the rest of us. They too have been made in the image of God. Children with autism may need therapy, medication, specific teaching methods, special equipment, and a whole host of other aids to help them learn and grow, but more than anything else they need love — especially the love of their parents.

"The sound of Noah laughing is like the sun bursting through the clouds on an overcast day"

FAVORITE RESOURCES

One of the most powerful and touching books about autism I have seen is the photo essay of children with autism titled ***Souls: Beneath & Beyond Autism*** by Sharon Rosenbloom. The photos and the passages written to go with them express both the beauty and the pain of dealing with autism. It also shows the humanity of these children so clearly through the autism. The children are beautiful and haunting. They remind me so much of Noah.

Doug & Michael

Ohio

Michael, age 8
Michael was diagnosed at 4 years

CONTACT:
Yogi1125@aol.com

BIGGEST CHALLENGE(S)

My biggest challenges have been three-fold:

In the 1st challenge we had to find out what was so unique about Michael. He is a twin and we knew something was different at age 18 months. It took us 2½ years to get our diagnosis! We ran from doctor to doctor pulling our hair out trying to figure out how to help him, but not knowing exactly what help he needed, as we couldn't figure it out.

Cornering our second challenge, trying to work with his public school system, proved to be just as daunting. They refused to offer all the options to us, and would not honor our wishes for services or support in his classroom. We had to hire an attorney to plead our case, which we won and then they still did not execute on the decision. The administrators and some of the teaching staff were lazy, ignorant, condescending, incompetent, arrogant, non-caring educators, from our prospective, and I am trying to be nice. We had experts lined up, willing to work with them and yet they still refused to listen to them or us. It was the old; "We know what is best for your son!" routine. They didn't even know him or know what autism was and still don't! Once we went to court, we ended up getting everything we had asked for all along, but they did not follow through on the court's decision. Their attitude was ridiculous. We have since pulled out of that public school system and found a much better way to have our son educated in a caring environment.

Help arrived as the third challenge was working its way to us with our State Representative (*Jon – great guy and fellow advocate*) who wanted to work with us to develop a task force to identify all the needs in the state and then advocate for those needs. The challenge was to convince the State Legislators and the Governor to create a Task Force and then develop recommendations. The Task Force was created and we came up with 43 recommendations. We are working our way through the recommendations until they are all enacted. In the meantime, there are kids and adults that are not getting the services or supports they need and it is extremely frustrating! I have become politically active to advocate for this cause. I do not like spending time on this, as I think everyone should just see the light, but they don't. Therefore, when I can, I have become an advocate for the cause for my son and everyone else on the spectrum in my state, as well as the country.

GREATEST BLESSING(S)

A true blessing in my life is not one person or thing, it is four people: My wife and three sons! My wife goes the extra yard to help Michael, as well as the other boys. We always find a way to get thru any situation, by either negotiating a compromise with everyone involved, crying, yelling, whining, laughing, or just taking a deep breath and starting over again. We are our own support group along with some friends, but as I have said for 25 years; 'You can count your true friends on one hand.' That has never been more true since we received the diagnosis. The diagnosis was actually a blessing, as we had finally figured out what we needed to do. It set us in motion to help Michael and we have been doing that ever since. You must rely on your own passion and drive to help your own family, as no one else will do it for you.

WORDS OF WISDOM

Early on I learned that in the immortal words of Jim Valvano, the great basketball coach at North Carolina State who died of cancer, who said: "Don't give up, don't EVER give up!" You cannot give up on your kids, or adults with autism. They need you more than ever. You must fight for the services, supports, and help that they need. You must help them to try to reach their potential. In addition, you must not be afraid to enjoy baby steps of success along the way. We enjoy our baby steps. One such baby step was at age 3. Michael could not speak, but we said to ourselves that one day we will have to tell him to stop talking so much. We achieved that moment about 18 months later! He hasn't stopped since and we thank God for that. Wow, baby steps, and we still laugh about it.

Love, compassion, passion, understanding, patience, challenging, engaging, emotional, persistent, and open to new ideas are all words you need to instill in your vocabulary. These past 6 years have been the most challenging and rewarding years of my life as I have added some new words to my vocabulary as well, such as autism. You need to remember when all else fails, trust your gut instincts on things. They are generally right on the mark – ours were! Please feel free to e-mail me with any questions or challenges you face that you think I might be able to help with. Good luck and God Bless.

FAVORITE RESOURCES

Autism Society of Ohio and Autism Society of America
www.Autismohio.org

"Love, compassion, passion, understanding, patience, challenging, engaging, emotional, persistent, and open to new ideas, are all words you need to instill in your vocabulary"

Erik & Nicholas

Missouri

Nicholas, age 6
Nicholas was diagnosed at 2 years

"From day one I wanted a son. A buddy who could share my interests in cars, tools and other "manly" things. You were born on April 30th, 1997, weighing in at eleven pounds and six ounces. My dreams for you expanded to being a football player that would make millions of dollars and be a big sports hero.

Your mother and I noticed that you didn't have much eye contact and you didn't talk or say words as other children your age were doing, but we didn't think too much of it until a Parents-as-Teachers coordinator suggested having you tested for a developmental disability.

You were diagnosed with autism and fell on the severe end of the spectrum. We didn't know what autism was but your mother researched it on the internet and read everything she could get her hands on. Meanwhile, I didn't think much of it because I had never heard of it, I didn't understand it and deep down wasn't sure I wanted to. After your mother had done her research and told me what she'd learned, we took a one month course from Judevine (www.Judevine.com) on how to work with you, help you reach your full potential and understand what autism was.

During this time I was in denial. I didn't support your mother and kept myself busy with other things to keep my mind off of your diagnosis. We tried everything reasonable (*diets, ABA - Applied Behavior Analysis, etc.*) to "get rid" of your autism to no avail. I blamed myself. I thought maybe this was all a result of my rowdy youth or that maybe God was punishing me for not being sensitive to people with disabilities as a child/teenager.

It took me a long time to realize that you were given to us for a reason — that we could handle it. Although you can be a challenge at times (*just like any child can*), I wouldn't trade you for the world. You are as strong as any football player, not only physically, but in your determination to succeed and rise above. Although things are different now in regards to what I thought we would do together, you are indeed my buddy. We love going for drives and listening to music together, having me make sad, mad, and happy faces and learning things from me that only a dad can teach you. We laugh and sing together. You will always be my boy, my son, who I'm so proud of and I will always love you."

To all the fathers out there who are first learning of their child's diagnosis, denial is always the first defense. My advice is to be there for your wife and child regardless and realize that although your vision of your child's future may be different than you originally thought, you need to support them, be their father and love them unconditionally.

"If a man does not keep pace with
his companions, perhaps it is because
he hears a different drummer.
Let him step to the music he hears,
however measured, or far away."
--Thoreau

Gary & Adam

Minnesota

Adam on his 18th birthday
Adam was diagnosed at 21 months

LETTER TO MY AUTISTIC SON

Dear Adam,

I wonder where you are today
we're holding hands but you're far away

Where do you go, what do you see,
what do you feel, when you look at me?

When you are sad and when you cry
It tears out my heart when I don't know why

I wish I could read your beautiful mind
to reach into your soul to see what I'd find

To know all of your thoughts and all your fears
to know the reason for all your tears

I know you love me, though you never say
you send me your feelings in your own way

You've made me the person that I am
A better dad and a better man

Thank you my son, you've strengthened my soul
you make me complete, you make me whole

Love always,

Dad

> The only challenge that comes to mind is coping with being apart from Adam. I have literally taken him everywhere with me whether it be camping, boating or a 650 mile road trip to Bass Proshops in Springfield, Missouri. He is my best friend...

George & Stephen

New Jersey

Stephen, age 10
Stephen was diagnosed at 2½ years

CONTACT:

georgegrahamnj@lycos.com

908-371-0195

BIGGEST CHALLENGE(S)

For me, the biggest challenge is helping my wife raise our 11-year-old son, Stephen, so that he will eventually be independent. He's our only child. Since he's moderately autistic, he doesn't have some of the issues that other children do. Still, he lags behind others. It took until about age 9 for him to wash himself in the shower. We're still working on him washing and rinsing his hair thoroughly. Little steps!

Stephen "helps" me fix things, including plumbing, and build things made of wood. I may have to hold his hand to help him use the wrench or hammer but I love the time we spend together doing it. He calls me at work every morning so we can talk. The reason? It's simple, Stephen can't really hold a conversation. We're trying to teach him to answer and make calls appropriately, then actually talk and answer questions on the phone. He's also learned to get dressed, set the table, and make his bed. All of that took time though!

Trying to get our son to act appropriately in public is a hit-and-miss issue. There are times he acts just like any other kid (*"I'm tired and want to go home!"*) and there are times he'll stand there giggling or reciting movie lines. (*Hint to parents with young children: listen to others and do NOT let your child watch movie after movie! They're telling you the truth and if you don't listen, you WILL regret it later!*) Although, we can normally redirect him.

Another issue is people talking to this 12-year-old like a baby. While his sentences are short and disjointed, Stephen is not a toddler. I talk to him like any other child of his age and so should you. That doesn't mean use every eight syllable word you know but it does mean don't raise your voice an octave and almost goo-goo. He's not stupid.

Stephen loves being on a bike so I tried for many years to teach him to ride one. He's a big boy so I had to get adult training wheels. He doesn't have the balance for this, or skates of any kind. After all these years, the solution to my problem was a tandem bike! Expensive? Yes! Worth it? Every penny! We ride all over the place as a family and he thrills to this adventure every time. He and I love the outdoors so we walk in the woods. Because of his extreme flat feet, he can't walk for more than 15 minutes at a time. Problem? NO! I bring the tandem bike along! When his feet start to get "tired" (*we call it that because he's afraid that if something "hurts" it means a shot from the doctor*), I sit him on the bike and push him along. Tiring for me? Sure. Worth it? You can guess that!

GREATEST BLESSING(S)

Some of the greatest blessings are the unconditional and complete love! Sure all parents have that when their children are little but parents with autistic children have it possibly forever. My son is kind-hearted and looks after others if they are being mistreated. More blessings are: Santa visiting our house a lot longer, being able to still hug and kiss him 'hello' and 'goodbye' for a long time to come, and the look in his eyes when I tell him I'm proud of him and love him. He's so happy to hear those simple words. It's a shame that many parents don't say these words to their children.

As strange as it may sound, another great blessing is caring people: those who try to understand our situation, who help us when we need it, who show their support and love to us as caring parents (*thank you Steve and Nancy*), and those who just listen when we need to vent.

Lastly, my wife is definitely a blessing. Using the different skills we both have, we've been able to help Stephen continue to grow into the wonderful young man he is. I certainly couldn't have done it by myself.

WORDS OF WISDOM

To me the key to raising an autistic child is to remember everything is "little steps." Even before I met my wife, I had visions of how my family was going to be. I was going to start to teach our child how to play chess at five and enjoy playing many other games like I did growing up. Well, once Stephen was diagnosed and I had come to fully realize his limitations (*which, by the way, I have to keep redefining!*), I had to adapt. First I taught him the names of the chess pieces. He caught on to that quickly! At about age eight, I bought a chess set which has the names of the pieces, arrows pointing the directions they can move, and numbers showing how far they can move on the front of each piece. Our son plays chess! Okay, so he doesn't know strategy (*although he wins more often than not*) but I have fun playing with him. What is the extra bonus of this? I'm making him use his mind more and more! I honestly believe between chess, checkers, and other games I have helped him progress. "Little steps." That's the way to go.

Don't expect your child to learn something the first time. Heck. Don't expect them to learn something the first 100 times! Just keep on trying and always, ALWAYS tell them how proud and smart they are! And you know what? I honestly believe it when I tell Stephen that. I'm always proud of all the progress he makes, every time he tries something (*even for the 100th time*), and every time he just tells me he loves me. Smart? Absolutely! Okay, so he's not an honor student. However, thinking back, he has learned more than I would've ever expected from him. I've learned never to think he can't do something. He always surprises me. Yup, "little steps."

> "My wife is definitely a blessing...
> I certainly couldn't have done it by myself"

41

Glen & Phillip

Texas

Phillip, age 3
Phillip was diagnosed at 4 years

CONTACT:
Through Glen's wife's website at:
www.laurasantos.com

BIGGEST CHALLENGE(S)

'What are you talking about?'

That was my reaction when my wife told me that our pediatrician wanted us to have our son evaluated for autism. Phillip was our first child so I didn't know anything was wrong. It wasn't until we had the teachers at his preschool fill out some questionnaires that I began to see that he was different from the other children.

But even then I didn't understand the path I was about to take. That would come after my wife and I decided we would take turns attending autism conferences. After my very first one, I knew that we were facing a long and tough adventure. When it was over, I sat in my truck and cried for 30 minutes before I could drive away. I wondered, 'how can I handle this; I'm not strong enough.' I spent the next two hours wandering around the walking trails at the Houston arboretum trying to get my thoughts together. I prayed for strength and I began to realize I had two options. I could allow myself to become overwhelmed or I could start working on a solution.

42

I've always felt that God had given me a talent for organization and details. I decided to use my abilities and immediately wrote up a document that contained all the information I had taken notes on during the conference, plus other information I found on the internet. I gave a copy to each family member. I knew we would have to have their support in order for any treatments to work.

I'll always be grateful that my wife stumbled on the DAN protocol at her first autism conference. Since that moment, we have been a team in our son's treatment. We've continued to attend conferences, and spent long hours researching the topic and talking to other parents. Recently, we organized and presented an autism awareness seminar at our church in order to help others who are facing the same circumstances. We rely on each other for advice and understanding; we work to keep each other going.

After three and a half years of treatment, Phillip has made great improvements. Our pediatrician (*who was the first to suggest we have Phillip evaluated*) has told us that today he would not catch the signs. During this time I have gotten down more than once, but have not wavered since I first made this decision to travel this road to recovery. It is every parent's dream for their child to succeed and not to suffer. We are willing to sacrifice ourselves to ensure their happiness. I often pray for guidance not only for myself, but for Phillip's doctors and educators as well. We all have a direct interest in his progress and we all need to support one another as best we can.

As for the challenges, my biggest has been picking and organizing the right treatments and tests for Phillip. We all have only limited time, money and sanity.

GREATEST BLESSING(S)

My greatest blessings have been the moments when Phillip speaks with absolute clarity. And I find myself just listening and hoping it will last. When I see him playing appropriately with other children, and when he gives me a hug with real feeling behind it are also a blessing.

WORDS OF WISDOM

Over the years, my words of wisdom have been simple: 'stick with it – it gets easier.' When we started treatment, I never thought I could do it, but now it has become second nature. I want to let everyone know that the struggle is worth it when you start to see real progress. Favorite quotes to get me through the day:

"There is one thing stronger than all the armies in the world; an idea whose time has come " - Victor Hugo

"First they ignore you, then they laugh at you, then they fight you, then you win " - Mahatma Gandhi

"The Lord is near to the broken hearted and saves the crushed spirit " - Psalms 34:18

Jamie & Harry

Massachusetts

Harry, age 3
Harry was diagnosed at 18 months

Casualties of War

I'm sitting in my living room on a cold January evening, listening to the wind and staring into my computer's blank screen. It has been well over an hour, but my mind won't budge. I'm working on the lyrics to the final song of an album that tells stories of parents raising children with autism. There are 11 songs in total; the first 10 were difficult, but they're done. This last one, however, is fighting me tooth and nail.

The song is about the traumatic impact that an autism diagnosis can have on a parent. The words swirl around me, but never come together. I sometimes come close, finding a phrase, even a single word. But when I begin to write, I'm overwhelmed. Every attempt is a glance into four long, painful years.

I remember sitting in a hospital room, staring down at a linoleum floor, while a cold voice says the words, "your son has autism." I see my son, strapped into a booster seat in our living room, a wooden shape toy on its tray. I'm kneeling before him, urging him to connect. "Hey Buddy!" I say, hiding a mounting panic. "Look at me! Where are my eyes? That's it. Good job!" I see a school administrator talking at me, my boy no more than a line item. I want to lash out, but heed our attorney's advice. "Never raise your voice. Ask questions. Gather data." The stress is unbearable.

I'm pulled from my trance when my wife returns home from a get-together with friends. I ask her about the party; she recounts a story from a woman whose brother had recently returned from a tour of duty in Iraq and was having a difficult time re-adjusting to civilian life. Apparently, he could no longer relate to those who were not there, who didn't understand what it was like to come so close to the edge, day in, day out. Her brother, she said, was a different person, distant, humorless... a stranger.

And there it was, the experience of raising a child with autism. It is war, struggling to stay sane in a world that has gone insane, and watching yourself slowly eroded from the strain of it. It is knowing that the life you once knew has been blown away, replaced by one in which you fight constantly, for your child's life and your own peace of mind; fighting insurance companies, school systems, unethical practitioners, bullies, even friends. It is trying to hold it together while people who have no idea how hard you're fighting give you answers without knowing the questions. It is the awful realization that you're alone, banished, different, adrift in a sinking rowboat, watching the world pass by on yachts, waving and wishing you luck. It is an urgent, desperate need for justice and retribution that you know will never come.

And so I wrote. I had found the elephant in my room; it was anger, overwhelming and fierce. I couldn't write the words because I couldn't bear to see them, to face the anger of a father of a child with autism. I was supposed to be my boy's protector, but I could not protect him from autism, and the problems that he would face throughout his life as a result of it. All I could do was fight. But that fighting, as it did for the soldier, had taken a part of me that I knew I'd never see again. It was innocence, the feeling that the world was filled with an endless string of beautiful tomorrows.

So here are the words that made their way onto the page, and became the song **"Surrender"**:

On the day the war began, I promised myself that I'd survive
And I've done everything I could, no matter what the cost, to stay alive
But the fighting's left me cold, afraid, and lonely
And I would give my life to come back home

I need you to show me one more time, I need to remember
Show me one more time, so I can get it clear in my mind
How to leave the past behind. If I can remember, maybe I can surrender

Moving angry through the world, I try hard to believe that nothing's changed
But that door has closed behind me, the damage has been done, I'm not the same
You're the only one who understands me. Only you alone can take my hand

I need you to show me one more time, I need to remember
Show me one more time, so I can get it clear in my mind
How to breathe and let it all go. If I can remember, maybe I can surrender

I am not the man I used to be. And I need your love to set me free

I need you to show me one more time, I need to remember
Show me one more time, so I can get it clear in my mind
How to find my peace again. If I can remember, maybe I can surrender

Writing this song, and the others on the album ***What Remains***, proved very therapeutic. Reading the words I'd written showed me that I had a lot of work ahead of me if I was to find some peace. But feedback from other parents has shown me that these feelings are real, and fairly common among parents raising children with autism. We are all casualties of war. And though it is a just war, and worth the fight, the experience changes us. We are stronger, wiser, and more resilient. But we are also sadder, more suspicious, and angry. Such is the price of war.

Jarrod, Hope & Molly

California

Jarrod & Hope

BIGGEST CHALLENGE(S)

Our biggest challenge was finding a doctor who actually knew what to look for.

I am a 40-year-old father, active duty military with over 21 years of service. I have four children, an 18-year-old son and 14, 9, and 5-year-old daughters. Recently, my oldest and youngest daughters were diagnosed with Asperger's. My wife and I have always wondered about our oldest daughter because of her odd behavior. Now, after reading up, it all has become clear. My youngest is the apple of my eye. I try not to show favoritism with any of my children, but she is the baby and a big-time daddy's girl.

My oldest daughter, always had problems in school and with behavior. She is a very sweet young lady and has had a rough time growing up. At one point, she was diagnosed as bipolar, obsessive compulsive disorder (OCD), ODD and Tourette's all at once. She's had all kinds of cocktails for medication. Some worked and some didn't. We finally found a psychiatrist who actually knew what she was doing and ran a battery of tests. It is finally a relief to actually know what her disability is.

She has been able to adjust, on her own, and with lots of therapy, but she also can have melt-downs. Plus, being a young lady, she can try your nerves. She knows exactly what buttons to push with my wife to get her spun up. We have learned that when this starts, we need to stay calm with her and try to figure out what has happened that day. Eventually, my wife can get it out of her and we are able to talk her through most anything.

We have had my youngest daughter, Hope, enrolled in pre-school since she was 18-months-old. She loved going to school and being around other children. She would have some meltdowns, but it was nothing to worry about. However, last year, the school said she was missing a couple of shots for kindergarten. My wife and I thought we had gotten them already, but we took her back, like taking a cow to slaughter, and ever since then her behavior has been radically different. She would kick, bite herself and other children, run away from teachers, and call her teachers names. Finally, she was kicked out of this very prestigious private school for kicking a hole in a wall when she had a meltdown. We put her in public school and an after-school day care. She had meltdowns daily at school but thankfully, the school noticed and started helping us out. She only lasted a couple of months at her after-school day care before we had to find other ways of watching her.

We took her to a psychiatrist (*the same one my oldest daughter went to*) and she did tests on her. When the diagnosis came back, it was autism. At first, I didn't want to believe it. There was no way. I thought, this is my fault. I was blaming myself for a lot of it. With my wife's persistence, I started reading up on autism and it finally hit me.

She acts like a normal little child, but all of a sudden, something will trigger her and she will have a melt-down. We are still in the process of figuring out what triggers this. Since I am on deployment right now, my wife is having to shoulder the brunt of the household. I am quite sure that she has figured out most of what triggers the melt-downs. I know this because my wife is a persistent and strong woman and very inquisitive. Maybe it is a male trait, but she will notice things I am oblivious to.

I am still trying to come to grips with two of my children having disabilities. I worry about them, and my wife's sanity, all the time. They are constantly on my mind. I wish I could be there to help my wife. What helps us out is that I am active duty and there are some programs we can use, once we get past the paperwork pile. But once I retire, we are pretty much on our own. I would like to retire so I can stay home and help my wife and be near my children more. Actually, I really need to be home more. But if it's the only way to keep my children in therapy and special programs, then I will have to stay on active duty.

I love my children more than life itself and I will do anything for them. It is hard because I am still learning all the aspects of autism. My wife constantly sends me articles, so I try to stay up-to-speed. If I could take away all of this from my children I would. But it is what it is. I love my children and I accept them for who they are.

GREATEST BLESSING(S)

My greatest blessing is having two daughters exactly the way they are. I would not change them for anything. They are a blessing and a privilege to have in my life. I just wish I could trade places with them.

WORDS OF WISDOM

As for something to tell other dads, I really do not have that much to say. This is still all new to me. Just don't ever give up on them.

Jason & RJ

Oregon

RJ, age 12
RJ was diagnosed at 4

CONTACT:
puzzledmedia@gmail.com

Reflections of a D.A.D. (Dedicated Autism Dad)

Looking back at the challenges I have faced as a father of an autistic son (*and there have been many*), the most appropriate place to start would be my becoming a father at all.

My wife, Angelene and I were married very young (*I was 19, she was 18*) and we both had plans for college, travel and all the other things newlyweds dream about. Five months after we were married, however, we received the news that we were expecting our first child (*there's a reason they say birth control is 98% effective*). Needless to say, that changed everything. We were at once, thrilled and terrified upon learning the news and we spent the next nine months doing our best to prepare for parenthood while learning to be married at the same time.

RJ (*Ryan Jason II*) had a smile that lit up the room. He was a very curious boy and the apple of my eye. Though he had severe ear infections throughout his first twelve months, he was meeting all of his developmental milestones until around 18-20 months of age. That was when he regressed into autism and we lost our son and his smile completely. (*Though it would take another two years of research on our part and a lot of lobbying to get a proper diagnosis for him.*)

After the challenge of learning to be a father and husband at age 20, my second challenge was coming to grips with the disappearance of my first born son and namesake. I didn't hear the word "Daddy" until our second son, Christian, said it some three years later. We were told initially that medication and possible institutionalization were our only long term options for RJ. All of the typical dreams a father has for his son were stolen the moment we received his diagnosis. Gone was teaching him to play ball, watching him from the stands as he led his team to victory, attending his college graduation – and the list goes on. At least those were my feelings in the beginning.

If RJ never has a family of his own and never passes on the name we share, I couldn't be prouder that he bears it. He has proven to be an inspiration to our family and to entire communities around the country. He has truly changed lives for the better everywhere he's been. What more could a father ask for in a son?

Along the way, my wife and I have had to overcome the ignorance regarding autism shown by doctors, educators, family members and total strangers. Fortunately, after having served as an advocate (*for my son and other families*) over the past six years, I've witnessed a tremendous increase in awareness and the progression of successful treatment for those on the autism spectrum.

Today, my greatest challenge is no longer in helping RJ along the road to recovery, but rather helping to change the paradigm of those inside and apart from the autism community. Overcoming ongoing ignorance can be a daunting task. I don't use the term, "ignorance," as a negative connotation towards those I'm referring to, but rather, as a statement of their lack of knowledge or understanding regarding the scientific evidence on autism that is available for anyone to see if they simply take the time to investigate.

By "ignorance" I mean: ignorance regarding a.) Proven scientific evidence regarding causation, b.) Treatments which are bringing about the recovery of tens of thousands of children and c.) The erroneous information doctors, educators and the general public largely base their assumptions on.

Despite these challenges, it encourages me greatly to see how far we've come, not only personally with RJ, but as a community. We now know beyond a doubt that autism is treatable and that there is hope for these children. I encourage you to visit the links that I'll be sharing at the end of my part in this great book.

GREATEST BLESSING(S)

The single greatest blessing I have had in my life (*besides my wife who is my best friend and soul mate*) was being given the responsibility of raising an autistic child. For starters, being a dad at 20 will show you (*and everyone around you*) what you're truly made of. You'll either grow up very fast or you'll become more of a child; insisting on your personal rights and being unwilling to give up your space, your time, and your toys. Add autism to that mix and, unfortunately, it's enough to send far too many dads packing. While I had to press through the childish inclinations at first, I chose to be responsible and to learn 'on the job'.

It was no picnic learning to share my space with a wife at 19, then with a baby at 20, then with a seriously stressed out child (*and consequently stressed out wife*) by 22, and in turn giving up my dreams of film school while working two to three jobs at once to make ends meet (*pumping gas, telemarketing... the abyss of forsaken dreams*) ...all in the name of "being a man." (*Fortunately, I was never bitter about it.*)

If RJ hadn't regressed, if he hadn't been diagnosed, I might not have grown up as quickly as I did. But because I did, my marriage became stronger and we were subsequently blessed with four more sons. Yes, I have five sons, and let me tell you; all of the head banging, screaming, feces finger painting (*Sorry – gross I know*), sensory issues, non-verbal communication, and every other blissful moment of raising a child with autism has made raising the other four a breeze in comparison. In fact, deliberately, purposefully, and successfully staring down autism with RJ has made most of life's stresses seem trivial by comparison. I like to say, "Never sweat the small stuff — and after autism, it's all small stuff!"

Not only has autism matured me and made me a better husband and father, it has also changed my professional paradigm and opened doors for me that otherwise might never have opened. Growing up, I dreamed of being a filmmaker. I aspired to be the next George Lucas, to wow the masses with my creative genius, and to one day give my acceptance speech at the Academy Awards. After becoming a father, I settled for broadcasting school, a career in radio (*and eventually television*) and somehow ended up with 12 years of broadcasting, sales, marketing and creative writing experience along the way. Little did I know that those skills would be put to good use in the world of autism!

My wife met Dr. Steven Edelson at a local conference in 2001. He in turn introduced us

to Dr. Bernard Rimland (*The "Father of Autism", Founder of ASA, ARI, and DAN!*) at a conference the next year. We went on to volunteer at DAN! and other conferences and I also did voice work for the Autism Research Institute over the next couple of years. In 2004, Angelene and I started Puzzled Media.

Today, I am a staff member of the Autism Research Institute. Puzzled Media has produced award winning films such as 'Recovered Autistic Children' (*which won a Gold Remi Award at the Worldfest - Houston Film Festival in 2005*). We continue to produce the Defeat Autism Now! online web casts which allow families all over the world to see the DAN! conferences in their entirety free of charge.

I may not have an Oscar on my mantle, but I have a son who is recovering from autism, and I have emails from parents all over the world who have been touched and who have benefited from the production work we're doing at Puzzled Media. If I never accomplish more than that in my lifetime, I've still accomplished more than I ever aspired to.

WORDS OF WISDOM

I'm just a guy who tries to do some good for those around me. I don't consider myself particularly wise as I work with the greatest minds in autism, but I do have battle scars, so I will humbly offer insights from own my personal journey.

Here's what I've learned in 14 years of marriage and 13 years of being a dedicated autism dad:

- Autism is not the end of the world; it's just the end of life as you know it.
- When you get married, you become the second most important person in your life. When you have a child, you're #3 and so on.
- You have to choose to be married every day; you have to choose to be a father to your children every day and you have to strive to do both better tomorrow than you did today.
- No one will ever be as dedicated to your child's advocacy and progress as you.
- Autism is a full body disorder, not a mental health issue. New information on causation, the medical needs of these children, and successful treatment are being discovered every day. Never stop learning all you can through your own diligent research and share your knowledge with as many people as you can! Also, video tape your child before, during, and after treatment if you can.

- Your doctor and your child's educators may have taken only one class on autism during one quarter of their entire educational learning process. Don't assume they know more than you do, even though they may think they do.
- Your extended family may know only what the evening news and *Dateline* have told them about autism. Don't assume they somehow genetically know what your needs are or what your child is going through unless you educate them.
- Your neighbors, people in the store, patrons at a restaurant or other parents at a school function probably don't know what autism is, let alone that your child has it. Overcome your burning desire to bludgeon them for their cruel stares and calloused remarks. If you communicate with them, maybe you'll enlighten them; if you communicate and they're still put off by your child, then they're in a darker place than you are.
- Always hold on to the hope that your child will recover and then take the necessary actions medically and educationally along the way to see that he or she does or at least has the chance to do so. If you fall short of complete recovery, you'll still be better off than if you had given up and done nothing.
- Pray hard and pray daily. Faith can move mountains.

Our family's best to you and yours!

> "Your extended family may know only what the evening news and Dateline have told them about autism. Don't assume they somehow genetically know what your needs are or what your child is going through unless you educate them."

Facts about RJ

- Typically developing from birth; chronic ear infections and colicky in first year.
- Was placed on antibiotics almost continuously for two years; continued receiving vaccinations on schedule while system was compromised from illness and antibiotics.
- Received extra round of vaccinations that was not noted properly by doctors in medical records.
- Following first MMR vaccination, "lights went out," – 18 to 20 months of age.
- For nearly two years, we were told it was a phase he would grow out of. Through online research of our own, we learned about autism and insisted that he be evaluated for it.
- Received diagnosis of PDD / Moderate function autism at age 4.
- Therapy interventions have included: Sensory Integration, Occupational, Speech and Auditory Integration Therapy.
- Nutritional interventions have included: Ambrotose complex (Mannatech), Mannatech 'Plus' (Endocrine system supplement), B12 injections, Super Nu-Thera (Kirkman Laboratories), DMG (Kirkman) and digestive enzymes (Kirkman).
- Future interventions will include: Full GI work-up and treatment, anti-fungal regimen, and transdermal glutathione with transdermal chelation therapy.
- RJ is now 13, has high function autism with moderately delayed speech and has been mainstreamed in school for the past two years with an aide. He received a standing ovation from the entire fifth grade class at his graduation to junior high.

Books:

EVERYTHING by Bernard Rimland!!!

Recovering Autistic Children (Revised Edition) – Steven Edelson, PhD, 2006

What Your Doctor May Not Tell You About Children's Vaccinations
– Stephanie Cave, MD and Deborah Mitchell, 2001

Unraveling the Mystery of ASD & PDD: A Mother's Story of Research and Recovery
– Karen Seroussi, 2002

Special Diets for Special Kids
– Karen Seroussi and Lisa Lewis, 2001

Children with Starving Brains – A Medical, Treatment Guide for ASD
– Jacquelyn McCandless, MD, 2003

Facing Autism: Giving Parents Reasons for Hope and Guidance for Help
– Lynn Hamilton, 2001

Evidence of Harm – David Kirby, 2005

And of course… *Autism: Heartfelt Thoughts from Mothers* – Judy Lynne, 2005

Websites:

www.AutismResearchInstitute.com – Autism is treatable. Learn how here.

www.DANwebcast.com – View all of the latest in biomedical and scientific findings regarding autism and treatment in streaming video and free of charge.

www.DANconference.com – Register online for the next Defeat Autism Now! Conference; twice a year (Spring – East coast, Fall – West coast)

www.GenerationRescue.org – Become a 'Rescue Angel' in your area and help other families looking for answers while learning more yourself.

www.Kirkmanlabs.com – In my opinion, the best nutritional supplement company I've come across.

www.Autism.com – Links to just about everything you'd want to know about autism, in several languages.

www.SARnet.org – The Schafer Autism Report – the most comprehensive and most read publication in autism. Find the latest in news, research and more.

www.AutismOne.org – Online resource and radio programming with shows produced by some of the brightest stars in the autism community.

www.PuzzledMedia.com – Puzzled Media's homepage with video samples of our work and more on who we are, what we do, and why we do it.

www.mannapages.com/all4RJ - Information on Ambrotose and Plus supplements exclusive to Mannatech. (*Note – We use the products only; we're not active in network marketing*)

Puzzled Media is looking for stories to share in future documentary films and videos! If you have a story to share, we'd love to hear from you!

If you have any questions, comments, rants or raves please email me!
Jason, Executive Producer, Puzzled Media, LLC

puzzledmedia@gmail.com
God Bless You and Yours!

Jeff & Josie

Wyoming

Josie, age 4
Josie was diagnosed at 22 months

CONTACT:
cgarner@tribcsp.com

My name is Jeff, I am the father of two wonderful little girls, one of which has autism. I have thought for weeks now, how I would write an essay about my daughter, Josie and our lives together. To be honest, I am winging it. I do know though, that my heart beats faster when I think about Josie; and if I am away from her I get the uncontrollable urge to run to her.

When we first found Christy was pregnant with our second child, we started planning right away. Christy got the room ready, I got every 'honey do' I could think of done, and we prepared our 3-year-old, Rylie, for the new baby. Josie was born on a sunny Friday morning in June 2002. She was a great baby with big brown eyes like her mom, beautiful dark skin like her sister, and her dad's temper. We had so much fun with her home. Rylie loved her sister and we were a happy family. Christy had concerns and tried to talk to me about them. I listened but inside, as husbands often do, did not think them founded and felt that Josie was just behind the ball and would gain fast. I was in denial.

Months went by and we were noticing problems more and more. My wife was moving into attack mode and was determined to figure this out. I was still in denial.

You know how you remember certain things, even small things in your life, very clear, very crisp? A certain bike wreck as a kid, the moment the minister says "I now pronounce you man and wife", or when the doctor says, "It's a girl". I remember clearly sitting at Children's Hospital, across the table from a nice lady who told my wife and I that Josie falls into the Autism Spectrum. What does that mean? My wife had mentioned autism, I knew the very basics. I knew Josie would come out of it, and I was still in denial.

Time passed, my wife continued to be the rock (*and the hammer*) for Josie. Reading every book she could, downloading every file on the internet, working to find the answers to Josie. I began to see more and more that Josie was certainly different, not only from her sister at that age, but kids much younger than Josie. We are a family that is often on the go, and having fun is important to us. The first time I really got scared about Josie and this bogus 'autism' diagnosis was at home. It was one of those memory moments again. I was home from work, Rylie climbing on my back attacking me with 4-year-old enthusiasm, Christy was holding me down so Rylie could get on, dogs were barking, and we were having fun. But Josie was not. She was sitting on the stairs, spinning a hair clip, totally checked-out. It scared me thinking 'so this is it', Josie would not know fun or live life.

Now, a few years later, with my wife leading the way, we are a family no longer struggling with autism, but living with it. Once I stopped trying to make Josie fit the mold of an average kid age, but rather progress day-by-day, step-by-step, life became good again.

With Josie, many people have a special connection. Mine is not all in what Josie says, but what she does not say. She is very quiet, and looking at me (*yes, still with big brown eyes*) she communicates with me. We are best friends, without saying a word. Josie is stronger than most people. I know Josie is going to be just fine.

I have two great girls and a wonderful wife. I have learned over the past few years we could not have a Josie without a Rylie and could not have a Rylie without a Josie. We are blessed, and with a positive outlook to the future, I know Josie will have a great life.

> "We have seen the best of people helping us and best of all, understanding us"

BIGGEST CHALLENGE(S)

I am sure my biggest challenge is understanding my daughter's needs. She communicates in all sorts of different ways, but sometimes we just do not know what she needs. A dad wants to take care of things and find the answer to all of the problems. I struggle with this. Josie will play and play outside and then tell me "hand hurt". I will look at it and see nothing so I assume she is just messing around. A few minutes later, she is screaming "hand hurt", then I realize her hands got wet and are freezing cold. Sheesh, I could have figured that one out! Why couldn't she just say, "hands cold"!

GREATEST BLESSING(S)

By far our greatest blessing is our family, friends, and therapists who have helped us along the way. We have seen the best of people helping us and best of all, understanding us. Our family has stepped above and beyond to help us live life as normally as we can and help us keep Josie out in the world, living life. Our friends have understood and have been a large part of Josie's life. Our friends' kids all play with Josie and help her along in a way that only other kids can.

WORDS OF WISDOM

Again, as a dad, I think it is natural to want to have all the answers. With autism, the sooner you realize that you are not always going to get them, the better. Autism truly is a puzzle and the pieces are lying all over the place. Try new things, keep things moving and focus on what works. Not everyone understands autism and realizing that will help as well. Tell everyone the truth. Autism cannot be hidden away and is nothing to be ashamed of. Most of all, do not feel sorry. Living with autism can be done – we are doing it!

> "Autism truly is a puzzle
> and the pieces
> are lying all over the place"

Jeff & Macklin

Illinois

Macklin, age 9
Macklin was diagnosed at 3

CONTACT:
jeffelbe@earthlink.net

BIGGEST CHALLENGE(S)

To be honest, I feel a little inadequate trying to write something like this. I don't know that I have anything to contribute, but so many others have done so much for us that I feel obliged to try to do something with the hope that someone will get something out of it that will help them. I guess that's the hard part, to try to do what's right, without really being sure.

GREATEST BLESSING(S)

We have three kids: Evelyn (1995), Macklin (1997), and Vivian (2000), and I realize everyone says it, but they are really good kids. When I can remember that, it's easy to be a good parent. Adrianne is the brains of our childcare/homeschool operation. I see myself as foot soldier, sounding board, and restorer of humor and patience. Without Adrianne or someone just like her I couldn't see myself as a homeschooler.

WORD OF WISDOM

I assume there are people who feel sorry for us because of Macklin's "problem." I have felt that as long as Macklin cares about us and wants our love our job is the same as any other parents. We have to teach him what he needs to survive in the world with whatever abilities he has or can learn and to try to help him into an environment where those abilities will carry him through the rest of his life. Other parents do this by sending the kids to college, or helping to start them in business, or getting them into an apprenticeship program, or just guiding and assisting until they are comfortable on their own.

Joe & Joey

Florida

Joey, age 21
Joey was diagnosed at 3½ years

CONTACT:
autismgym@aol.com
www.autismgym.org

BIGGEST CHALLENGE(S)

To see my son communicate, and for us, to live a long life for him and my daughter.

GREATEST BLESSING(S)

My greatest blessing is my family, our health, and the fact that we get through the hurdles in life.

WORDS OF WISDOM

Keep your family close to you, love them, life is truly too short.

407·234·7456
www.autismgym.org

In the year 2000, Joe's wife started Autism Gym. Feeling like she had nowhere to go and that there were no other families like their's. She simply went to the local recreation center and asked for one night, one hour to start a gym program so kids like Joey could play together and parents could talk. Almost 7 years later, they are 300 families strong and a non-profit organization. Their plans are to get their own building so they can be open every day!

Joel & Danny

Maryland

Danny, age 4½
Danny was diagnosed at 2 years

CONTACT:
joelsimon@comcast.net

I am the father of a 4½-year-old boy with autism. He was diagnosed in the summer of 2004. We also have a 6-year-old typical child. Our family is Jewish. Every year, I send greeting to my family and Jewish friends around Rosh Hashanah, the Jewish new Year, which occurs in the Fall. Our faith teaches that Rosh Hashanah is a holiday, where one takes stock of their life from the previous year. For nearly a decade (*since e-mail became ubiquitous*) my greeting was short, very short. Last year, I did something completely different. The following is an edited version of last year's message:

"Sorry to disappoint some of you (*DP that's you*), but this year's New Year's greeting is a little different. The reason is this year has been a little different. This is the end of the first year with Danny's diagnosis of autism. It is a year that, to say the least, has caused me to take stock of my life, and the essence of life in general, more often than ever. In some ways, I feel Rosh Hashanah may be a little redundant.

This past year, I cried and laughed simultaneously more often than I did in my previous 43 years of life combined. To see the joy and promise of a bright, generally happy three-year-old is such a high; to see the shackles and frustrations brought on by autism is such a low. Deb and I, particularly Deb, have worked hard to release the shackles. The 35+ hours of weekly therapy, the diets, the vitamins, and the rest have lead to tremendous progress. Danny is talking in phrases spontaneously, learning to read words and count, and reducing his tantrums. We so often see the light of Danny shine through; perhaps, that is why it is so frustrating that we have not yet propped the door open so the light can flow freely. We will continue to work to be sure. We will continue to fight the educational and medical insurance bureaucracies to ensure that Danny receives the services that have helped him progress so much this past year. We will continue to search for additional therapies and services that will allow Danny to fulfill all of life's promises.

Speaking of Ellie. She has been so wonderful this year. She is blossoming (*there is no better verb*) into a magnificent little girl. She is a loving and caring big sister who wants nothing more than to be loved by her little brother. One of my biggest frustrations through the year was seeing the disappointment in Ellie when Danny could not respond to her in the way she sees her friends younger siblings respond to them. Danny has made strides in this area, and Ellie is more understanding than most 5-year-olds; but, we are not there yet. That

said, I am so proud of the person Ellie is becoming. Just last week Ellie's great-grandmother gave her a small check for Ellie's upcoming birthday. Ellie was told she could get whatever she wanted with the money. Ellie pondered her options for a moment, and said she wanted to give it to Tzedakah to help the people in New Orleans. Her caring and compassion left me speechless (*and you know that is no easy feat*).... "

> "To see the joy and promise of a bright, generally happy three-year-old is such a high; to see the shackles and frustrations brought on by autism is such a low"

Joel & Timmy

Illinois

CONTACT:

joelkogen@ameritech.net

BIGGEST CHALLENGE(S)

My name is Joel and I live in the Deerfield, IL area. I have a little boy who is 7-years-old who has autism (DX code 299.0 and non verbal). His name is Timothy, but we call him Timmy for short. He was diagnosed in 2002.

Around 2001 my sister, Suzy, who has a son a year older than Timmy, said that she thought Timmy did not seem to be developing in a normal way. I initially disagreed with her and said, "Suzy, I would know. I've worked as a special education teacher's assistant for 5 years." I also mentioned to her that I had worked as a part-time recreational aide and as a camp counselor for a summer camp program. I felt as if I would know if he had disabilities since I had training and experience working with children.

Timmy had been to the pediatrician shortly after birth and he reported that he did not foresee any developmental delays. We later moved and Timmy saw a new doctor and this doctor did not recognize any developmental issues.

When we moved again a few years ago and we told the doctor there about my sister's concerns, he referred us to a neurologist. The neurologist ran tests and found nothing abnormal. The neurologist then referred us to a genetics expert and a physiologist for testing. While the genetics testing was inconclusive, the physiologist felt as if there were some problems.

Although it was difficult, I eventually acknowledged that Timmy did have some developmental issues. We found an early intervention program through the Northern Suburban Special Education District (NSSED). With the help of the NSSED early intervention team we found the Jewish Children's Bureau (JCB) Center for Young Children with Autism. Timothy stayed in that program from age three to six. When he became too old to be a part of the program he transitioned to the NSSED Education and Life Skills (ELS) program.

GREATEST BLESSING(S)

Our greatest blessing is the progress that Timmy is making all the way from the JCB Program to the NSSED ELS program. We are grateful to all of his private team members and his school team members.

WORDS OF WISDOM

First of all, love your child. Don't ever neglected him/her. Secondly, remember that your child is a child first. Let them be a child. Third, for therapy, it is best to have your child do every kind of therapy out there; ABA , Floortime, TEEACH, etc.

For the dads who are still married and having a hard time with this, a family a therapist is helpful. It also may be a good idea to have your own session without your wife.

Favorite Organizations:
JCFS Center for young Children with Autism - www.jcbchicago.org
The North Suburban Special Education Distract - www.nssed.org
The North Suburban Special Recreation Association - www.nssra.org
Glenkirk - www.glenkirk.org
Little City - www.littlecity.org
Lambs Farm - www.lambsfarm.org/

Website References
Msn Groups Autism Community Dedicated to making a Difference
        (*Joel is the Assist Manager*)
Autism spectrum Disorder Support Group
Autism support Group & Parents of kids/adults with Autism.
Yahoo Groups
Catalog Resources for the Special needs (Joel is the list owner of this Resource)
        http://groups.yahoo.com/group/catalogresourcesforthespecialneeds/
Children with Autism
        http://groups.yahoo.com/group/children_with_autism/
Floortime - http://groups.yahoo.com/group/Floortime/
Illinois CAN Chapter - http://groups.yahoo.com/group/illinoiscanchapter/
Autism Society of Illinois - http://www.autismillinois.org

John & Noah

Wyoming

Noah, age 5
Noah was diagnosed at 4

CONTACT:
john@jcsposse.com
http://blog.myspace.com/smalljourneys

BIGGEST CHALLENGE(S)

There is one thing we take for granted every moment of our life. We do it every few seconds and it often escapes our concious thought. In fact, since you have began reading this you have already done it at least a few times. It is breathing. Sometimes we forget that we are doing it. Seemingly unnoticed every couple of seconds we fill our lungs up with air in order to live. I am as much a biologist as I am a member of the Village People so I am not quite sure how the science of breathing works. I don't know how the oxygen passes through my body and into my brain. I am certain however that without doing it I would go the way of the unicorn. I also know that if I don't breath enough air I get dizzy… and I know that air is invisible...and that if people breath too much they can hyperventilate... and that the air in bigger cities smells like my uncle. That's not very much knowledge for something that I depend on thousands of times per day is it? I don't respect how many times I have breathed in my life without anything going wrong. I cannot remember an instance during my 32 years that I have opened up my mouth in search for air and not being able find any. It is unimaginable to ponder how many times I have breathed in my life. Millions of times this invisible substance has saved me without a thank you or much of an acknowledgment on my part. So right I want to give a special shout out to the O2 for keeping my skin away from turning a yucky shade of blue.

Keeping me alive is not the only thing that breathing has done for me. Air has been my tonic for mental health as of late. When times get rough, I spend a moment and just breathe. When stress arrives unwelcome as a vacuum salesman at my door, I don't react; I just take in air and focus on letting my breathing soothe me. Yes, it sounds a little Zen coming from a guy from Wyoming but it has made a difference for me.

I stole this idea from one of my favorite TV shows, *LOST*. One of the main characters,  Jack, counts from one to ten in his mind when he faces a crisis. I liked that so much I started to use the 10 second count in my life as well.

For those ten seconds I allow myself to be overtaken by whatever emotion is poisoning me. Whether it is fear, anger, frustration, or other similar negative feelings, I let them have power over me as I breath and count. During that ten second intermission, I just inhale and exhale and when I reach the number ten I take control of my feelings. This saves me from saying or doing the wrong thing by just reacting to the situation in front of me. In fact some of the greatest revelations I have had lately have come during those 10 seconds of airtime. I think maybe a good example would fit in nicely here:

A couple weeks ago, my family and I were shopping at Target. I am one of those parents who dreads taking my kids to public places. Anytime we go to a restaurant or a movie I spend what seems to be several hours prepping my children like they were pilots from the movie *Top Gun*. We have meetings and strategy sessions on how to behave in public places. I do this so our family is seen and not heard when we are out among people. I don't like to make a commotion. I don't like making a spectacle. I simply want my family to gently flow in and out of places without leaving a wake of destruction behind us.

This drive of mine to have a angelic family is most certainly bathed in stupidity. I need to get over worrying about what other people think of our family. I need to understand that when you have little boys you are going to make a scene regardless of what planning you have done. I need to realize that when you have a six-year-old with autism and a three-year-old with a social agenda, being a traveling noise machine is part of the deal.

Anyway, my autistic son, Noah, has been doing so great as of late. We used to not be able to take him to places like Target because we were terrified he would run away or want to experiment with some laundry detergent on the store floor. Thankfully, those days have been behind us for a while now. Noah has just held our hand and been a total superstar the last few times we have brought him. This trip was different as he was having a bad day. I should have known this but I didn't recognize it until it was too late.

My wife, Jenni, and I split up as soon as we entered Target. She took Noah and I took my typical three-year-old, Riley. About five minutes into my shopping I heard the storm begin. I recognized a series of short high pitched bellows that I knew were coming from my sweet autistic son. Noah had not had a serious fit in over a year but my wife and I knew it was coming and there was little we could do. Within moments he threw a temper tantrum that could be heard in the hidden alien colony on Mars. His crying was so loud it sounded like he was right next to me. He was so upset and I felt terrible for him and Jenni. Noah's screams were as if he were being tortured by some unseen force and nothing could be done to stop it. I started to move in their direction as fast as my 5'3" legs would take me. By then, the other patrons started to take notice of his loud cries echoing inside Target. Since I was not with my wailing son, it was clear nobody thought I was his father. This allowed the other shoppers a freedom to let their thoughts be heard. With my three-year-old, as I followed the screaming, I started to hear the others speak.

"My son would never get away with that!" was the first comment I heard from a girl picking out some shoes.

To be honest it hurt a lot...so I started to count and breathe. 'One' I thought.

Then I heard an older lady speak the classic mantra of the ignorant outsider: "What kind of parents would not be able to control their kids?"

I wanted to turn around and at least give some sort of crusty look that a character from *Beverly Hills 90210* would appreciate. This lady did not know a thing about our son. She did not know he was autistic. She did not know that when he got upset he was unable to calm himself down. She didn't know my wife and I have worked tirelessly on his therapy, that we have forsaken so much money, time, emotion, and life just to get him ready for kindergarten! That lady had no clue how much my wife loved him. If she had known these things, perhaps she would have curbed her tongue. She, however, just assumed it was all the product of bad parenting.

Since I was still only on the number four, I just kept walking. I reminded myself to keep breathing.

The next comment shot into me hard. "What a cry baby! Waaaahhhh!" laughed some guy in a leather jacket.

I went from feeling slight embarrassment to rage. What kind of person says something like that about a little boy? I am not a fighter by any means. I am not brave. Moths frighten me. However, I wanted to tackle this man and make him eat every dog biscuit he had in his cart. No doubt he would have pummeled me into marshmallow fluff. But I still wanted him to pay for making fun of my defenseless child. Instead I exhaled and thought 'six.'

I inhaled again and went from walking to jogging toward the sound of my weeping son. I did think, at one point, how great it would be if one of these people would just offer to help or at least give a smile of encouragement.

When I hit eight in my mind, I saw my wife carrying Noah in her arms. I saw tears sliding down his bright red face. I had made it to ten and I was no longer angry or hurt by what anyone else in the store had said. I was only concerned for my wife and my heartbroken son.

My wife and I made an escape plan for them to get out while I continued our shopping. Their entire walk out of the store was sound-tracked by my little guy's wailing! My wife, with a stride of courage I am not sure I possess, walked boldly past the self-righteous audience and out the front door. When I no longer heard his cries, I knew they had made it out to the parking lot.

I stopped for a moment and began to think about what had just happened.

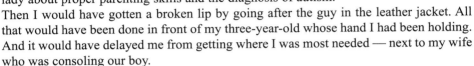

What would have happened if I would not have counted? I would have probably spent five minutes arguing with the old lady about proper parenting skills and the diagnosis of autism. Then I would have gotten a broken lip by going after the guy in the leather jacket. All that would have been done in front of my three-year-old whose hand I had been holding. And it would have delayed me from getting where I was most needed — next to my wife who was consoling our boy.

Spending those moments just breathing and not reacting allowed me to have a moment of inspiration as well.

How many times in my life have I been like those people? How many times have I stood in line at the grocery store and thought something about the person in front of me? How many times have I acted judgmentally about a situation someone else was in?

Standing there in Target, I realized I was just like those folks who were so cruel. I probably would have thought the same thing if our roles were reversed. I need to live my life with more empathy. I need to put myself in other people's shoes more often. I must be the person in the store who would offer to help or at least give a smile of encouragement. In short, my ten seconds of air time taught me I must become a better person.

Breathing is good for the body and the soul. It helps us to take a moment to just think without reacting out of emotion.

My son Noah got over his tears within a moment once we made it back home that day. I, however, will never forget the ten seconds I spent breathing in Target. I hope I never will.

> "I did think, at one point, how great it would be if one of these people would just offer to help or at least give a smile of encouragement"

Ken & Kanta

Colorado
(originally from Japan)

Kanta, age 6½
Kanta was diagnosed at 4 years

CONTACT:
otome5739kc@gmail.com

BIGGEST CHALLENGE(S)

I know my son has an ability to learn. To let him learn, everything needs to be individualized. We have to think how to motivate him, how to make him understand, how to keep him concentrating.

The cost of therapies. He takes speech therapy once a week. It is a 30-minute session. Although I want him to take it twice a week, we cannot afford it. We even had to stop his occupational therapy due to the high cost we cannot afford, and we are doing it on our own. There are many alternative therapies we would like to try. Almost none are affordable. Family Support Funding can cover only a part of speech therapy. We just have to think it is better than nothing.

Many people misunderstand my son unless they know us better. Not only his symptom but also his ability.

Greatest Blessing(s)

While doing a search, I learned that many famous people are (*were*) under the autism spectrum disorder (ASD). So those people are models (*goals*) for my son, although we are not sure he can be one of those people.

I have more friends through meetings for parents with ASD child(ren). I probably could not, if it were not for my son. I'm involved in a couple of discussion groups.

We could find many neighbors who helped us. They understand his problem but are still willing to let their kids play together.

Words of Wisdom

This is my son… I cannot say more than that.

Kanta, age 7

Mark & David

Texas

David, age 18
David was diagnosed with Aspergers at 15

CONTACT:

markdebc@comcast.net

When you were little David, I marveled how your mind worked – and I often wondered what you were thinking and why things were so very different from the world that I knew as a boy. I now understood why I was made so passionate. I always cheer for the underdog, the guy who works and works until the day comes when justice and the moment of sunshine breaks through. Even David's grandfather, my father, deeply ingrained it in me when he chased and ran down some bullies through a park and alleys to show those brutes that they could NOT treat his son and friend that way. I understand my life and how much I love you.

You were born with TAR (*Thrombocytopenia, Absence of Radius*) syndrome, missing radius bones in both forearms. We received professional and compassionate services from Texas Scottish Rite Hospital for ulna bone centralization during your early years. Overcoming the surgery and having casts on your arms for your first few years of your life seemed to be the big hurdle. We marveled at your ability to "scoot" around on your bottom with those casts, and later splints, during those early years.

TAR syndrome was what I concentrated on, but then your mother and I noticed your incredible and different ways – playing and perfect aligning of toy cars and your lack of eye contact. As you grew, there was Lego, long hours of building Lego, and avid hours of video and computer playing. I thought my wonderful son was just a shy, deep thinker with an engineering-type mind (*my profession is civil and general engineering*). In elementary school, teachers were amazed at your intricate art-work and "Dictionary Dave" abilities.

Then, the biggest challenge came with middle school and high school with a greater emphasis on social interaction. You "parallel played" by yourself in the elementary school yards. In looking back I thought it was a phase and that over time your social skills would change. However, I was wrong and ignorant. I underestimated how society and people respond if one socializes in a non-neurotypical way.

Your birth in 1987 and the clinical DSM-IV category of autism spectrum (AS) (299.8) in the year 1994 made it likely that you would fly under the radar, invisible, just like autism is "invisible" to the human eye. You did, because you are such a fine, quiet, gifted young man. The late self-diagnosis (*your mom's friend said maybe "it's something they call Aspergers"*) occurred when you were 15.

This huge challenge of social interaction, missed non-verbal cues, unnoticed glances, eye movement, voice inflections, use of words and how people interact was something I could not grasp in its totality and impact. With time, upheaval, struggles during high school and challenges in my own personal and family life, I discovered the blessing of the autism spectrum. Like a blazing fire, I applied my engineering skills to knowing more about autism and the autism spectrum. With research and meeting other families, I learned why the autism spectrum is "invisible" and how varied it impacts them.

My understanding of the autism spectrum now is what gives me confidence. It brings me incredible joy just being your father. As a little boy, you typically used the word "hope" in your prayers and conversation. It was "hope Grandpa", "hope I do", "hope I study", "hope our dachshund Misty" — I tried to rephrase your sentence or encourage you to try another verb, but you persisted.

Within the autism spectrum world, it makes sense that you used the word "hope". It is every parents "hope" to seize the deep, simple, rich qualities and being, of their loved one. My son is my "hope". He has shown me how the world is and how "hope" is the very center of what autism is. A "hope" that comes with each passing day, like a stream our lives flow over smooth and jagged rocks, beautiful and clear. I look forward, more than ever, to sharing and growing with my son.

Mark & Erik

North Carolina

Erik was diagnosed at 4 years

CONTACT:
markeide@markeide.com

BIGGEST CHALLENGE(S)

My biggest challenge was learning about autism. I never heard the word autism before my son was diagnosed with autism at 4-years-old. My heart fell to the ground. I was lost; not knowing is the worst thing. I searched for everything I could find and still did not know a lot. I was looking for something that said it could be fixed. But nowhere did I find it. I felt lost and sad. Not knowing what to do or what I should do. It was hard on my marriage. Finally, I found the strength to pick myself back up and move forward. My son was not dead, just a little slow in some things. So I worked on his strong points and made them better. I learned about his weak points and worked with my son to bring him up to speed with other kids his age. Now Erik is doing very well in school, reading is his passion. I hired a private tutor to help bring him up-to-speed.

I am lucky. Erik is reading, writing, doing math, bike riding, running, and playing with other kids. I feel in my heart that he can live a normal life. Erik wants to go to collage and become an animal veterinarian. He knows he needs to do well in school to make this dream come true. Erik also wants to get married and have kids.

Erik is only 12-years-old and he knows more about what he wants and is working harder on it than I was at 12-years-old! Erik sets his mind on something and can stick with it. So in the beginning, I was lost and not sure what was going to happen. Now I know Erik can make things happen on his own and with my help.

GREATEST BLESSING(S)

Erik has the kindest heart, everyone who meets Erik says he is the sweetest boy. I am amazed by it, because at 12-years-old, I was not that sweet. Erik wants to please everyone and being mean to other kids and friends just does not happen. So I am blessed with a sweet son.

WORDS OF WISDOM

Get involved, there are a lot of groups out there. You are not alone. I was afraid at first to mix and meet other parents, get over it and mix and meet. There is so much support and help out there, it is waiting for you. Once you start meeting others and start to find this help, you will want to start to do what you can to help like I am doing with a web site, and the fathers group and dads and sons groups. You can enjoy life and get involved.

Mark & Holly

Canada

Holly, age 7½
Holly was diagnosed PDD/NOS at 4 years, 10 months

BIGGEST CHALLENGE(S)

My biggest challenge is trying to determine the best programs and treatments for Holly. We have tried biomedical treatments such as the GFCF diet, Probiotics, and Chelation therapy. We have utilized programs such as ABA (*Applied Behavior Analysis*) therapy, Sensory Integration and Speech Language pathology. Although some parents have found significant improvements in their children with the above treatments or programs, we have had limited success to date. There seems to be a never-ending stream of "experts" with the "cure" for autism, but when I speak with other parents, I find very few children are making significant improvements. I want to do the best treatments and programs for Holly — I just don't know what are the best for her.

Greatest Blessing(s)

My greatest blessing is having a strong family support system. I have a strong marriage and close ties with my family. Both my wife and I are firmly committed to doing whatever we can to support Holly. I have met many single parents with autistic children. I understand how the stress and uncertainty associated with autism can tear families apart. I feel very lucky to have someone with whom I can discuss Holly's needs and who can be there when I feel overwhelmed. I think every father who has children feels overwhelmed at times.

> "Both my wife and I are firmly committed to doing whatever we can to support Holly"

Words of Wisdom

Love your child. If you truly love your child and accept them as a blessing, they will feel that love and respond accordingly. There are times when I wish Holly was as affectionate as her younger sister, but I have found that the more affection I give to Holly, the more she will give back. I also believe you need to have a sense of humor. Holly had started unplugging my clock radio every day. At first, I was getting angry because I had to reset the time and alarm every night before bed. Then, I decided that this is not such a big deal. I started to laugh as I walked into my room and saw the numbers flashing on the clock. After a few weeks, I got in the habit of expecting a flashing clock, and I got a chuckle each time I saw it. She has since stopped doing this, but now I have the proper mind-set for Holly's next "misadventure".

Marty, Ryan & Hunter

Missouri

Ryan was diagnosed at 19 months
Hunter was diagnosed at 3 years

CONTACT:
mopar1@centurytel.net

BIGGEST CHALLENGE(S)

My biggest challenge is accepting their autism.

GREATEST BLESSING(S)

My greatest blessing is having two beautiful boys that God has given me, even with the ASD (*Autism Spectrum Disorder*), they humble me and I feel that I have become a better person because of them. I feel they are truly God's children and a worry that I don't have is that they have salvation guaranteed when it is all said and done.

WORDS OF WISDOM

Don't look at the negative – live day-by-day. Put everything in God's hands and enjoy them.

> "I feel they are truly God's children and a worry that I don't have is that they have salvation guaranteed when it is all said and done"

FAVORITE RESOURCES

The best resources change based on the need at the time. We have used Judevine www.Judevine.com (*in Missouri*) and they have helped us in many ways along the journey. Also, we have the Department of Mental Health. Our service coordinator is wonderful and is very compassionate about advocating for our boys. Impact also has an expert that has trained us on special education law. Your needs change as they grow and behaviors change. The internet provides all of us easy access to various resources. I just would advise to call, ask, and be honest about your families needs when doing so.

Matthew & Breanna

Australia

Breanna, age 4
Breanna was diagnosed at 6 years

BIGGEST CHALLENGE(S)

My biggest challenge is making people understand what autism is. Autism awareness is very low. People think that autistic people can't talk and are these mathematical geniuses (*shown to us through the movie Rainman*).

However, there is a broader spectrum to how autistic people are and how they behave. I want people to learn to accept my daughter for who she is. We don't need to cure them, we need to love them.

GREATEST BLESSING(S)

My greatest blessing is that we are from a Christian household and that our faith can help our family with any situation or challenge put before us. I have a loving wife, and a daughter who is beyond her years in her help and understanding of her autistic sister. Thank you to my wife Nikki and my daughter Kiera. I hope that her brother Dylan grows up with the strength and understanding that she has.

Words of Wisdom

Listen, read, learn, encourage, love. Listen to what other people have to say about autism and their experiences. Read as much as you can. There is plenty of great information out there for people to use. Learn from these people whether from what you have heard or what you have read. All this information will help lighten the load, and if you find something works for you then share it.

Encourage your family as well as others with an autistic family member. Sometimes even fathers need a shoulder to lean on. We have to be pillars of strength for others so that in time when we need them, they can be there for us sometimes.

Love your child with all that you have. This love brings patience, joy, kindness, gentleness, self-control and understanding. We need all these elements to help our children.

> "Sometimes even fathers need a shoulder to lean on"

Why

Why didn't I cry when they told me the news?
Why didn't I feel sad?
Why did I not hold my wife's hand?
Why did I not FEEL?
Why was this like something long ago?
Why had I heard these things before?
Why did I feel comforted?
Why did I not feel alone anymore?
Why did I feel that I had discovered me?
Why did I feel that I knew you from before?

Because

Because when I was younger I was different
Because as a child I did the same
Because my emotions are bottled
Because I don't know how to show them
Because I don't feel part of this world sometimes
Because the child I was is the child you are now.
Because I accepted you for what you are
Because I didn't cry, I just understood

Tomorrow

Tomorrow is another day that we help each other to grow and understand ourselves more and more, not to be like others, but to co-exist with others, trying to love them as they would want us too. Together always.

One day

One day Bree, we will fly.

Miguel & Nicholas

Massachusetts

Nicholas, age 5½
Nicholas was diagnosed at 29 months

CONTACT: kunfoo@aol.com

GREATEST BLESSING(S)

The greatest blessing that Nicholas has given me is that he has changed my outlook on life. You see, I have 3 other wonderful children besides Nicholas, a beautiful 26-year-old daughter Christina, another beautiful 20-year-old daughter, Michele, a handsome son, Michael who is almost 19, and as you can probably guess I love them all very much.

Watching them grow up I remember so many times when I felt so much pride and joy as they accomplished things such as first steps, first words, first days of school...along with so many other things I cherished those moments. But with Nicholas I feel that way about him at least 100 times a day! Because with his situation (*autism spectrum disorder - ASD*) even the smallest accomplishments are huge! I use to think scoring a goal in hockey or soccer or even runs in softball was such a big deal, and it is...but now I get so much pride and joy just watching Nicholas play with his toys! He has brought out such a tremendous, blessed love out of me and I have never felt so much pride nor have I ever been happier in my life!

I also would like to mention a little something about my beautiful wife, Alessandra. I feel that I couldn't have been blessed with a better wife. If I wrote down all the things I'd like to say we'd have to write another book. I must say I am in awe of her and the way she is with our Nicholas. When it comes to being a mother & son, she and Nicholas are truly a match made in heaven.

I guess what I'm trying to say is that I appreciate my life, my wife and children so passionately now and that's the blessing that my little Nicholas has given me! (*Thank you Nicholas...daddy loves you!*)

BIGGEST CHALLENGE(S)

The only real challenge I feel is that I want to be here for him as long as I can be. I just want to live forever for him and make sure he is always okay, safe and happy. I know that can't happen, but my wife and I have already discussed taking much better care of ourselves, eating better, more exercise, more check-ups – all so we can try to stick around as long as we can! As far as everything else like his education, life plan, financial needs, that's the easy part, not that it may be always easy, but its what we can control, and I feel doing things for him an honor. I love him so much I consider it a blessing to have Nicholas as my child. If that means I have to work hard to get him what he needs so be it, its a blessing he's my child. God chose me for him, I'll always do my best for him. I feel we will have a wonderful life meeting those challenges as a family.

WORDS OF WISDOM

You grow up, you have a career, you get married, have children, then grandchildren, you get old and sit back and all you can think about is the proud and loving moments you had with your children and grandchildren; the playing, the laughing, the look on your beautiful bride's face, the kindness of your parents and grandparents, and family get-togethers.

When you have a child with ASD, you also think about the special bond that you have with that child where they are constantly fighting their problems with communication, socialization, etc. Yet, still show you so much love and joy words can almost not express how much! Basically, my words of wisdom are that life goes by so fast, appreciate and cherish what you have every day – make memories – love the blessings that God has given to you, your loved ones, your family, especially your child with ASD who is the biggest blessing of all!

Nicholas is just 5 and a silly, wonderful, loving little guy and was diagnosed with Pervasive Development Disorder/Not Otherwise Specified (*PDD/NOS*). He is doing great thankfully and in a full-time ASD (*Autism Spectrum Disorder*) classroom where he receives ABA, speech therapy and occupational therapy, along with lots of play time and socialization too.

> "I just want to live forever for him and make sure he is always okay, safe and happy"

Mike & Lucas

Ohio

Lucas, age 7

CONTACT:
mioanes@woh.rr.com

BIGGEST CHALLENGE(S)

There have been a lot! Constantly having the patience to deal with Lucas, when he has tantrums, doesn't want to go along with plans, won't dress himself, or just stops to pick up a bug when we're barely on time for an appointment.

Getting the right placement for him in school has taken a lot of time and basically insisting that the school system "do the right thing."

Getting the right diagnosis — Asperger's. The psychiatrist that saw him for a couple of years 'just couldn't see it,' but a father of another boy with Asperger's who we met in a store could. An occupational therapist who saw him for the first time recognized it, but the social worker/therapist who'd seen him for years couldn't.

Being in the dual role of "dad" and "grandpa" both.

GREATEST BLESSING(S)

Again, there are many blessings:

- The people we've met, parents and volunteers in the Challengers baseball league he was in this summer. The good doctors we've finally found to help him, through Cincinnati Children's' Hospital.

- The strangers in many public places who will stop and listen to his stories or look at whatever object he wants to show them.

- Lucas's innocence, fantastic stories about China, Harry Potter and making potions.

- Doing "kid things" that I wouldn't without a seven-year-old in my life.

- Camp Nuhop, for being a welcome place for Lucas.

WORDS OF WISDOM

Don't be afraid to tell anybody your child is autistic, but don't (*and don't let the child*) use it as an excuse. Conversely, when Lucas has met and is playing with kids, like in a park, if things are going well, I don't feel a need to tell anyone.

Lucas was initially diagnosed as bipolar shortly before his fourth birthday. We thought something wasn't right, but thought more of his symptoms fit those of Asperger's. His first psychiatrist wouldn't diagnose him as having Asperger's because Lucas made eye contact with him!

Mike, Eddie & Mike

Pennsylvania

Mike & Eddie were diagnosed at 2½

What you imagine life to be and what life actually is are two different things. We all know that… we all had visions of what it was like going to be a father. Whether you were having a son who was going to be the next all-star quarterback for the Eagles or a daughter who would grace the covers of *People Magazine* as one of the 50 Most Beautiful in the world, we had it all planed out. Me? I was doubly blessed in October of 1997 when my twin sons, Mike and Eddie, were born. I not only had a quarterback, but the wide receiver as well.

Besides your normal concerns of a new father such as how am I going to afford twins and will I ever get another night of sleep again, life was going well. The boys grew and developed and I remember the excitement I felt the first time they walked and said "Dada." Yep, things were going as planned and I started thinking about who should be the quarterback and who should be the wide receiver. Unfortunately, real life seems to get in the way of our best laid plans. Just after the boys turned a year old, my wife noticed they were not longer saying "Mama" and "Dada," as a matter of fact… they were not saying much of anything. We started to notice some other things: no eye contact, compulsive jumping, not interacting with anyone. My wife started to have some concerns and I did what any good father would do… deny, deny, deny. I assured my wife that everything would be okay, the boys were just being goofy and it was a phase. Everything will be fine, and besides, this wasn't in my plan so it can't be happening.

Another year had past, and my wife's concerns continued to grow. Even I was starting worry, the boys just acted differently than other kids their own age. But, our pediatrician assured us that there was nothing wrong, we heard they were "boys," "twins," and since they were born 6 weeks premature they might be slightly delayed but they would catch up. Once again, I felt I had to be the voice of reason and assure my wife that the boys were fine, even though deep in my heart I knew they weren't. During this time my third son Timothy was born.

A few months after Timothy was born my wife, Sue, read an article about autism and it described the symptoms Mike and Eddie had to a tee. We changed pediatricians, saw a developmental specialist, and were given the diagnosis of autism. My quarterback and wide receiver have autism… it should make for some interesting huddles. I went through all the stages… denial, anger, resentment, and pity. I am still waiting for acceptance to kick in, it has been over two years and it hasn't happened yet.

Mike and Eddie are five-years-old now; to play catch with them is still a goal I am working on obtaining. They continue to amaze me some days and frustrate me the next. I watch them run around playing and jumping in our backyard and think to myself "everything is going to be okay" and then some behavior will pop up or a social outing turns into a disaster and I think that I should never leave the house again. Good days, bad days, good moments, and bad moments. That is how we all live now and we keep chugging along.

Has my vision changed for Mike and Eddie? Yes, and no. With all the hours of therapy they receive every week, they are the hardest working five years olds I know. They work more hours a week than I do, but don't tell my boss. They now say "Daddy" among other things, and each word they say or behavior they learn is a victory. We have all worked very hard to get them where they are and will continue to do so. I used to have their whole lives planned out and now I don't know what tomorrow will bring. What I do know is this, just because Mike and Eddie have "special needs," doesn't mean my role of a father changes. I am here to look out after them, provide for them, and make sure they get all the things they need so they can live the fullest life possible. I also know that the roles of Mike and Eddie haven't changed. Some of the greatest joys of my life have come because of things they have done. They are my sons; I am proud of them and love them. Besides, when it is bedtime and I have to wrangle them for bed they can have the best "deek and jive" moves I've seen since Randall Cunningham. Maybe there is hope for my football dream yet.

Monty & Daniel

Arkansas

Daniel was diagnosed at 2 years, 3 months

BIGGEST CHALLENGE(S)

- Trying to put frustration and anger into positive energy so that I can be my best for Daniel.
- Putting up with Daniel's mom. (*Smiles*)
- Figuring out ways to teach Daniel things so he will understand us and this world.
- My job requires being away from home frequently and I don't get to spend a lot of time with him.
- Accepting that I have to change the whole way I was raised to be able to raise Daniel. As of this time we still can't do the father and son things I was looking forward to such as camping, fishing, and hunting because of the safety issues. But we do have fun playing trains, cars and trucks, and video games.
- Worrying about taking care of Daniel by myself if something happens to his mom.

GREATEST BLESSING(S)

- Daniel is full of love and hugs and kisses.
- He is so creative that he gets in way too much trouble. (*Smiles*)
- Daniel is amazing! His computer skills blow my mind.
- I am 40-years-old, and I rely on common sense to make it in life. Daniel is 8-years-old and he can already read better than most high school graduates I know.

- Daniel has hyperlexia, so reading and spelling are a breeze for him.

> "Open your eyes to see what great things your child can teach you"

WORDS OF WISDOM

- Educate yourself about autism. Research the information yourself to find what is going to be the most beneficial for your child.

- Open your eyes to see what great things your child can teach you.

- Do what you can to advocate for your child.

Patrick & Travis

Ohio

Travis, age 9
Travis was diagnosed at 2

Travis was born on August 20, 1997 into a nice, middle-class family. The Leave-it-to-Beaver kind of family where dad goes off to work in the morning and mom stays home. We were a mid-western family that ate dinner together every night at 5:30.

Travis seemed to be a healthy, robust, perfect little baby boy. Our first child, a girl we named Victoria, was healthy. We had no reason to think that he wouldn't be healthy as well. His mother, my wife, Julie, did everything right during both of her pregnancies. She didn't drink or smoke. She ate well, took her pre-natal vitamins and followed the orders of her obstetrician to the letter.

Everything was supposed to be perfect and it was, for about a year and a half. That's when things started happening. He stopped talking. He became sullen and seemed unhappy most of the time. His doctor referred us to Early Intervention. It was there that the "A" word was mentioned for the first time.

After the diagnoses of autism, we went through the Denial-Anger-Grief-Acceptance cycle that every one goes through when given dire news. However, I'm not sure we got to the "Acceptance" part. Actually, we consciously decided to not accept it. We decided that he was broken and if he was broken, he could be fixed. We read books, we went to doctors, we put him on a special diet. We did everything we could to "fix" Travis and he only seemed to get worse. He stopped speaking completely. He had trouble sleeping. There were times when I went to work with only one or two hours of sleep. Worst of all, Travis just seemed miserable.

We took him to a doctor in Cleveland. The only thing he did for us was prescribe the drug, clonidine, a blood pressure medicine that had the side-effect of helping Travis to go to sleep at night. We took him to doctors in Cincinnati. They helped a little as well, but there was no changing the bottom line. Travis was still autistic. He wasn't getting fixed. I didn't realize it at the time, but during all of this, I built a little box deep down in my heart and I started putting all my fears for Travis in it. "Will Travis ever talk?" Stuff that in there. "Will he ever sit in a regular classroom with normal classmates?" Stuff that in there too. "What will happen to Travis when Julie and I are too old to take care of him?" That one was the worst fear of all. Stuff that one way down in there.

I kept my little box locked up and was able to keep from asking myself these questions. I told myself that it was counter-productive. I had to keep my mind on the here and now. I had a job, a wife, a daughter, a home and a special needs son who needed to be fixed. I had no time for this, I told myself. It worked for awhile, then I went on a "Walk to Emmaus".

A "Walk to Emmaus" is a non-denominational Christian retreat that is designed to build Christian leaders. When my friend asked me to go, I quickly agreed, thinking that, if nothing else, it would be a good break. A chance to collect my thoughts, re-group so-to-speak. I was not at all ready for what happened.

A Walk to Emmaus features long periods of time spent deep in prayer and meditation. This is difficult for some one who has a box locked up in their heart. Slowly, the box was opened and the fears were unleashed. I sat crying in the sanctuary of the First Methodist Church in Sidney, Ohio on a Saturday afternoon. Fear was rampant in my heart. "What good is this doing me?" I wondered. "This is exactly why I keep this stuff locked up!" echoed in my mind. "How am I going to..." I was so busy wallowing in self-pity that I almost missed it.

"There's no autism in heaven."
"What was that?" I asked myself.

> "There's no autism in heaven"

"There's no autism in heaven." It was crystal clear and came from somewhere other than me. "There's no autism in heaven." There it is again. Suddenly, I envisioned Travis, glorified, his mind free of its terrible affliction. He spoke to me. He told me that he loved me and his mother and sister and that he was sorry that he couldn't say it before. I told him that it was okay and that I loved him too.

Then I envisioned myself with a big hammer, smashing that little box to bits. There was no need for it anymore. There's no autism in heaven.

Since that day, we've continued to work hard to help Travis, but I don't try to fix him anymore. I have learned to love Travis for who he is. We're also busy raising our daughter who's now eleven and has braces on her teeth. We still eat dinner as a family every night at 5:30.

Travis has made strides in some areas. He has gotten no better in others. He still doesn't talk or sit in a regular classroom, but it's okay, because I know in my heart that, in the long run, he'll be fine. Some day he won't be a square peg in a round world. He'll speak and laugh and experience true joy. I know this because there's no autism in heaven.

Paul & Anders

Colorado

Anders was diagnosed at 4½

CONTACT:
970 668-4985
Pcm185@aol.com

I drove up the driveway, got out of the car and there it was, standing on the front porch steps. The beat-up little yellow truck. One of the older kids must have left it there. I looked at the little yellow truck and I got a lump in my throat. Then the tears came. I picked up the little yellow truck, sat down on the steps and started crying.

Anders was conceived in late 1998, one week before I went in for the snip. Three children was enough we thought and we were not getting along well and on the verge of getting divorced anyway. Anders had other ideas and we believe that HE wanted to come into our family. Since his two older sisters and older brother were born after uncomplicated pregnancy and deliveries, my wife wanted to have the baby at home. With the help and coaching of the mid-wife, I delivered this beautiful, healthy, happy baby boy in August of 1999. We named him Anders. Anders is a not–uncommon Scandinavian and German name. In German it also means "different." How true that would prove to be.

Anders was happiness personified. He was always laughing and smiling and happy and loved to cuddle and be cuddled. He was a bit delayed in speech and walking but he is a boy and he does have three older siblings who were quite happy to do everything for him. At age 2-3 I began to become concerned about his development since his speech was not developing normally and he was showing no interest in potty training. His motor skills were also lagging behind. My wife was in denial and would always say " He is just different and he will decide when he wants to speak and when he wants to use the toilet. You should honor the child that he is." But others noticed too and a friend, who is a counselor, suggested he might be autistic.

At age 3-4 he started to regress and would no longer say words that he used to say clearly and appropriately. Add the stress in our marriage and a move and Anders withdrew. At age 4½ I finally convinced my wife to have him tested and the diagnosis was Autistic Spectrum Disorder with suggestions for therapies and treatments. It was, in many ways, a relief to know what it was and somewhat how to proceed but also rather frightening at the same time. A month later I found the little yellow truck on the front porch. I turned the truck over and spun the wheels. That was probably the most that Anders would ever do with it. He probably wouldn't ever run around the yard with it going vroom-vroom. He probably would never fill it with dirt and sand and dump it and it was then that I realized that I had lost my little boy. Or better said, I had lost the little boy that I though I had. And I cried.

I grieved for him. I grieved for our family. Mostly I grieved for me. I had to take the initial step to get Anders an IEP (*Individual Education Program*) and put him in school. We home-school the other children but the preschool teacher at the local elementary school was a special-education teacher and they had an Occupational Therapist (OT) and an Speech Therapist (ST) on staff so he could get therapy a few times a week. He responded well but when school ended so did therapy so we found an OT and an ST on our own and also put him in Hippo therapy which he loves. Because of his age he would have had to go to Kindergarten this year so we elected to keep him at home, continue with private therapy and spare him the sensory assaults of the classroom. He seems to be responding well to music therapy, directed play by the OT, and a great listening program from the ST. He has said "papa" and "love you" which makes me very happy. He is still not really verbal but will grab my hand when he wants something and pull me to it and communicate in that way. The hardest thing for him is when he is mad or frustrated because he cannot communicate that except for scratching and pulling hair. My wife discovered when he gets like that, getting down on his level, looking him in the eye and asking "are you mad?" seems to verify his anger and calm him down.

He loves to be outside, especially in the wind, enjoys skiing (*the learning process is mostly trial and error*) and walks and riding in the bicycle trailer or in the bike seat. He can ride his own bicycle with training wheels, loves the swings and is fascinated by airplanes and helicopters. He is also unbelievably warm and cuddly and loving and affectionate. We love our Anders with all our hearts and are trying hard to rise to the challenge that he brings to our lives. My goal is to make his life as productive and as rewarding for him as possible.

BIGGEST CHALLENGE(S)

Having had to convince a reluctant spouse that her child is not in the range of "normal" and needs special help has been the greatest challenge, followed closely by convincing her that labels can be helpful and early intervention has the greatest chance of success. Every marriage has it's own challenges and I am sure we are not alone in trying to deal with the monumental additional challenges that an autistic child brings.

> "We love our Anders with all our hearts and are trying hard to rise to the challenge that he brings to our lives"

GREATEST BLESSING(S)

The three older children have been the greatest help imaginable. To them Anders is just Anders and they accept him for what he is and how he is with absolutely no reservations and with unbounded love and affection.

The next greatest blessing we discovered much later after talking with other parents of autistic children. Anders eats everything. He has an enormous appetite and will usually eat anything and everything placed in front of him and would root around in the kitchen and pantry searching for something to eat all of the time if we would let him.

Thanks to Judy for putting these books together so that we may share our thoughts.

Paul & Johnny

Florida

Johnny was diagnosed at 2 years

CONTACT:
veli06@bellsouth.net

"JESUS I LOVE YOU, BLESS ME TALK"

As a Catholic Priest, marriage and children were not part of the plan. So it was with nervousness that I left active ministry and entered married life in 1988. My wife Judy and I decided to wait a few years before having children. We planned, prepared and prayed, and after a smooth pregnancy, Johnny arrived on December 28, 1992. A perfect, cute and cuddly baby.

My paternal instincts kicked in early on and like any proud father, I cherished that bundle of joy. When Johnny was about 18 months, we thought that he had a hearing problem. His pediatrician was not concerned. When Johnny was about two, we noticed that he was not "talking" like other children in Judy's "Mommy and Me" group. His new pediatrician suggested a developmental evaluation. The psychologist, while administering the test, said, "to rule out autism."

That is the first time in my life, I had heard the word autism. I went home and looked up the diagnostic criteria for autism in DSM-III, and there it was. Johnny had all the main characteristics for an autism diagnosis. First, I did not know what to make of it; I did not anticipate its implications. I thought he would be cured after some speech therapy. I was overwhelmed and confused. I shed a few tears. I was in denial.

While some parents we knew frantically pursued services for their autistic children and complained about their sad plight and predicted catastrophes for future, we took a laid back approach to the situation, always hoping that "it will all work out for the good." My God-experience has a lot to do with how I deal with Johnny which I shall explain below.

As for "challenge/blessing" ratio, Johnny is a 10/90. He is such a loving and lovable child, a pleasure to be around, despite his antics and obsessions. His obsessions such as eating ice, rewinding tapes just to watch the credits of movies, although distressing, very often bring tears of joy and sadness at the same time. At age 13, he has the innocence of a young child. He loves to kiss babies wherever he finds them: in the mall, in the pool, at the park, etc. While the parents of babies wonder why a grown boy who appears to be "normal" would do this, I have to always explain that he is autistic. When they hear that, most parents are willing to let him kiss their babies. The fact that Johnny has no external signs of a disability is both a blessing and a curse, because I have to always explain his behavior to those who expect "normal" behavior from him.

Johnny is a happy child. He does not ask for much, his needs are very limited. When we go out, as long as he gets his French fries and a coke, he is content. I take him to a mall nearby and he has to make five stops: Dillards to ride the escalator, the Disney Store to look at the DVDs, Walden Books to flip through some children's books, and Burger King for his fries and coke. At the end of that routine, he is delightfully happy. When I don't permit him to ride on the "choo choo train" (*due to his age and size*), he complies without complaint. However, during a rare temper tantrum, it is heartbreaking to watch his frustration to express himself in words. In those moments, I sigh deeply and implore the Universe to rewire his brain, hoping against hope for a miracle!

While people might look at Johnny and say, "what a sad situation," Johnny is not even aware of the complicated lives such people live. He is "happy in his own world". I am a firm believer that each person has to be happy "only in his or her world." We should not impose our criteria for happiness into other people's world. That has been a very comforting thought for me in dealing with Johnny's disability.

As I mentioned above, my faith has everything to do with the way I deal with Johnny. I have never been angry with God or complained to God, asking the proverbial question:

96

"Why Me?" Instead, I ask: "Why not me?" Life has no guarantees. There is no law that I should be spared of all difficulties and others should suffer. Considering what has been happening in the world, and the pain and suffering that more than half of humanity suffers through on a daily basis, my "cross" is easy to bear. This ability to have perspective and see the "big picture" has been of enormous help.

I never believed that Johnny's autism is a punishment from God, although it was implied by some "god-fearing people" because I left the priesthood and thus, according to them, betrayed Christ. The story of a man born blind in the 9th chapter of John's Gospel answers this dilemma for me. When the disciples asked Jesus whether it was his sin or that of his parents' sin that caused him to be born blind, Jesus said: "Neither. It was no sin, either of this man or of his parents; rather, it was to let God's glory show forth in him". I am not able to explain in words how that glory is manifested, but Judy and I always feel, that there is something about Johnny that is a special and glorious blessing for us. Ironically, the name John means, "gift of God".

The book, *Autism and the God Connection*, by William Stillman, has confirmed my conviction that Johnny is in my life to teach me about the mysterious ways of God. As the author asks, "Isn't it plausible that the person with autism comes into the lives of

the parents who need him most, deliberately and by supreme design?" My deep faith in the providence of God makes me believe that some day, in God's time, Johnny will improve his comprehension and talk. Ever since he was able to repeat words, I taught him a prayer, and Johnny says it every night when I put him to bed. "Jesus, I love you, bless me talk." I tear up when I hear him say that prayer. I also have special moments with him in church. I hold him close to me and place my hands over his head and pray that Jesus unleash his healing power to make him whole.

Another book that has been of tremendous help is *The Power of Now* by Eckhart Tolle. He talks about the importance of living in the "Now" and not being worried about the future. Uneasiness, anxiety, tension, stress, worry and all forms of fear are created by too much future and not enough present. So I make a deliberate attempt to live in the moment, enjoying and being grateful for what I have today, rather than what I don't have. One of my favorite passages from Mathew's gospel where Jesus admonishes his disciples not to worry gives me great strength and hope: "Look at the birds in the sky, they do not sow or reap, they gather nothing into barns; yet your heavenly father feeds them. Which of you, by worrying, can add a moment to his life span? Stop worrying then, your heavenly father knows all that you need. Enough then of worrying about tomorrow. Let tomorrow take care of itself; today has enough troubles of its own."

Yes, I don't worry about the future, but that does not mean that I don't plan. God has given us a brain to use it for navigating through the exigencies of life and I use it not to obsess but to make reasonable plans. I pray as if everything depends on God, but I work as if everything depends on me. I have basically three plans for Johnny's future. They are called the "Mommy Plan," the "Tommy Plan" and the "Daddy Plan." Mommy Plan is that Judy will take care of Johnny well into his adulthood. Judy is currently 42 and Johnny is 13. If the Lord gives her another healthy 35 years, she can take care of Johnny in the home until he is 48. After that, "The Tommy Plan" kicks in.

His younger brother Tommy, who is 11, is a wonderful brother to Johnny. I believe that the Lord placed Tommy in our lives to be of help to his brother. Tommy is a brother, mentor, teacher, protector and whole lot more to his older brother. A few years ago, Tommy said: "I am not getting married until Johnny is no more autistic." When I asked him why, he said; "What if the girl I marry does not want to take care of Johnny?" I had tears in my eyes. I have no doubt that Tommy will support and love Johnny throughout their lives. They have a special bond. I never stay awake thinking about his future or being anxious about it. It will all "come out in the wash" as one of my favorite clients always tells me. I am 55 and so the "Daddy Plan" is to have a good life insurance policy.

We are also blessed with an awesome community of parents in our area. Many have paved the way and fought the battles, and we have benefited immensely with a great education for Johnny, family support and an e-mail group list called "Denise's List" that keeps us up to date with current legislation, upcoming events, parent support and resources.

As a hospice chaplain, dealing with death and dying on a daily basis, I am consciously aware of the fragility of life and the futility of fretting about what lies in the future. As Eckhart Tolle writes in *The Power of Now*, "Future is an imagined now. When future comes, it comes as the 'now.' When that 'now' arrives, the answer, the strength, the right action or the resources will be there when you need it, not before, not after."

In the meantime, I just enjoy every moment with Johnny, his smile, his playful innocence, his obsessions, quirks and all. I stand in awe before the unfathomable and mysterious ways of God, in total surrender, experiencing the peace that transcends all understanding, and thanking God for our blessing, Johnny!

Phil & Jake

North Carolina

Jake was diagnosed at 18 months

BIGGEST CHALLENGE(S)

- Finding appropriate places for Jake's education that I felt comfortable with.
- Putting Jake in a home.
- Staying a step ahead of Jake in his new and weird habits he keeps coming up with.
- Finding different things to do with Jake that he will enjoy.
- Dealing with uncaring and incompetent people who are suppose to be taking care of Jake.
- Spending hours child proofing something and Jake figures it out in three minutes or less.

Greatest Blessing(s)

- Jake will be in heaven with me and he will be able to talk about all the things he couldn't on earth.

- Seeing Jake fall down on the floor and want to be tickled for the last eighteen years.

- Jake still wanting to go for a horseback ride on me even though he is bigger than me.

Words of Wisdom

- It is a long life, don't try to cure everything the first year.

- If there were to be a cure for autism everyone would know. It would be on CNN, ABC, CBS, etc.

- Watch how your child reacts to their caregivers. They will let you know if they are comfortable with them.

- When they are young you think they will be with you forever, but most kids grow up and leave home.

Randy & Gavin

Wisconsin

Gavin was diagnosed at 3 years

BIGGEST CHALLENGE(S)

The first challenge that I had to face was accepting the diagnosis of autism. When Gavin began showing signs of autism at around the age of two years, we had simply thought that he was going through the "terrible twos." In fact, the first doctor that we took him to had said the same thing. That took me to the next challenge. I was at the bottom of the learning curve about autism. Where could we get factual information about autism and who could really help us? It was then that I learned that the parents must take on the task of making all of the decisions about the treatment of their child. This may appear to be obvious, but it is very challenging if you consider that both the short term and the long term benefits of the child must be weighed. Also, making these decisions is a very dynamic process. Some of the treatments produce almost immediate results and others require time. This will impact how you decide what treatments to abandon and what to continue. This made it difficult for me as my background deals with direct, quantifiable results. However, in dealing with treatments for autism, much of the measurements used are very subjective. All of this took me into an area that I was very unfamiliar with.

When parents make the treatment decisions, they often find themselves at odds with health care providers and insurance companies. That is because as their child's advocate, they will act in the best interest of their child, no matter what the cost may be. Battling with these third parties requires perseverance with little guarantee that the services will be covered. A family's finances can be stretched quite thin when they must pay out-of-pocket for non-covered services. Dealing with the behavior of an autistic child can be very taxing on the entire family. This is especially true if the child is non-verbal, as Gavin is. We do not have the same perspective on our surroundings as the autistic child has. With all of this taken into consideration, I have found that my biggest challenge is having enough patience. There are times when many parents of autistic children feel as though they are facing insurmountable odds. It is then that we all must realize that we should obtain the help where we can find it, both for ourselves and for our children.

GREATEST BLESSING(S)

Although the challenges facing parents seem overwhelming, the blessings are also there. It may be easy to complain about the burdens placed upon us, but it is much more beneficial to have an attitude which embraces hope. How can I benefit from all of this? What can I learn? How can I grow? In which ways can I help other parents?

In helping others, you will also help yourself. You can network with other parents and they can often get you through those tough days. You will learn to get the help wherever you may find it. There will always be those who don't care much about your child's welfare as well as those who are in it strictly for the money. Once you learn to make this distinction, finding the appropriate help should become easier. So the greatest blessing of all will be the talented and compassionate individuals who will come into your life to help your child.

I cannot emphasize enough the need for parents to "think outside the box". The many treatments for autism are in a constant state of flux. Many of these treatments are being refined as the body of knowledge continues to grow. Our paradigm of autism continues to change day by day. Look at what happened about 40 years ago when Dr. Bernard Rimland challenged the prevailing theory that autistic children were caused by "refrigerator mothers". A revolution was started! As these children's parents, we are on the cutting edge and we can make a difference. Remember, that your child is unique, like all of us are. The fact that they are autistic does not change this. The following quote is from the opening chapter in a book written by one of my favorite authors, who was an economist.

WORDS OF WISDOM

"If men were like ants, there would be no interest in human freedom. If individual men, like ants, were uniform, interchangeable, devoid of specific personality traits of their own, then who would care whether they were free or not? Who, indeed, would care if they lived or died? The glory of the human race is the uniqueness of each individual, the fact that every person, though similar in many ways, possesses a completely individuated personality of his own. It is the fact of each person's uniqueness-the fact that no two people can be wholly interchangeable-that makes each and every man irreplaceable and that makes us care whether he lives or dies, whether he is happy or oppressed."

The Logic of Action Two by Murray N. Rothbard

Rick & Bryce

California

Bryce was diagnosed at 22 months

CONTACT:
r-midmail@pacbell.net

BIGGEST CHALLENGE(S)

No one really knows what causes autism, and no one can give you a prognosis of what a likely outcome for your child will be. This is a haunting reality. I see some families at autism functions that look like death warmed over. Although I have never lost a child, I sympathize with people who have lost a son or daughter, because our son's regressive autism is not unlike "losing" part of our child.

GREATEST BLESSING(S)

Whenever I visit Children's hospital, I get a harsh dose of reality. As desperate our son Bryce's situation is, there are other children who have it a whole lot worse.

Although, we don't know what will eventually be in store for our child, we have chosen not to resign ourselves to whatever fate has in store. We chose to try to educate ourselves and influence the outcome in whatever positive way we can.

In this process, I have seen my wife take on the project like a mother bear defending her cub. The "blessing" in this, is the girl I fell in love with years ago has won my heart many times over.

WORDS OF WISDOM

There are a lot of value judgments that you will make as a parent, and as a family. Our observation was that our pediatrician (*who is an honest, great resource for our typical developing child*) had nothing to offer when it came to autism. We have made a choice to use our pediatrician as a sounding board, to evaluate risk from any alternative treatments, and educate ourselves so that we could best utilize bio-medical interventions in conjunction with ABA therapies to help our child.

For what it is worth, this early intervention has made a difference for our son. I recommend the book *Children with Starving Brains* by Dr. Jaquelin McCandless, and

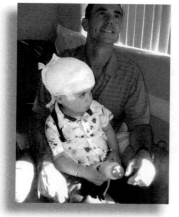

recommend that you meet with a DAN! Physician to discuss their protocol. The Center for Autism and Related Disorders (*CARD*) is light years ahead of their peers in ABA, and if you are lucky enough to have one nearby – you should contract services with them.

Final words of wisdom: We have met some extraordinary, dedicated people in the field, and the tendency is to trust and believe that the school district is similarly motivated to offer a program that is designed for your child's individual needs. Don't believe it.

You have rights as a parent. Possibly the most important decision you can make is to pursue independent educational evaluations for your child. By law, if you disagree with the District's assessments of your child, Independent Educational Evaluations (IEE) must be provided "in all areas of suspected deficit" at public expense.*
The independent assessments proved critical for us in securing services that were not offered at the time of the initial Individual Education Plan (IEP).

(or the Districts must file for due process to show their assessments were appropriate.)

Rob, Robbie & Harrison

Maryland

Robbie was diagnosed at 4 years
Harrison was diagnosed at 3

BIGGEST CHALLENGE(S)

Toilet training! I tried everything! Make a fake mountain with a potty on top to motivate them to go, a "Johnny on the spot", etc. I tried putting them on 7-15 times each day, giving candy, and timing them. I sometimes got angry or frustrated. I tickled them so they would laugh. I used warm water and even wrote poetry about using the toilet. I thought if my boys could be involved in some competitive sport, then they would be motivated to use the toilet. My older son is urine trained. As for Harrison, he never quite made the connection and always gets mad when I say it is time to go to the bathroom. So, we continue to work with both boys. Robbie is more difficult to bowel train as he was born very early at 26½ weeks and with no large intestine (*removed at 18 days due to necrotizing enter colitis*) his stools are liquid. We keep trying with him too.

GREATEST BLESSING(S)

My greatest blessing is having two sons that I truly love and truly love me back in their own way. My boys do not mind the way they are as they know nothing different. They usually make eye contact with me and seem to make choices although I am not always happy with their choices. Both boys are able to indicate to me whether or not they want to do some activity. Then there are the times when my older son comes up to me and says, "I love you, Daddy" and then gives me a big hug. That is my greatest blessing. At those times, he seems almost like a normal kid. It just makes me feel great and needed that he is able to say that to me, not often but often enough.

WORDS OF WISDOM

Take care of yourself so you are not too hard on your children. Try not to get upset with your kids but work with them to be the best they are capable of being. Planning is the key, especially planning for activities that will keep your children busy and motivated.

"My boys do not mind the way they are as they know nothing different"

Roger & Katie

North Carolina

Katie, age 27
Katie was diagnosed at 3

CONTACT:
919-304-9065
genrog@mebtel.net

I am the 72-year-old father of Katie, a 27-year-old adult with autism and mild cerebral palsy. She was born January 16, 1979 when the world was barely out of the dark ages of "blaming" refrigerator Mom's for autism. Can only Mom's be refrigerators? Our first problem was finding out what was wrong with our beautiful girl. My wife, Genie, and I saw many things in Katie that were worrisome such as not making developmental landmarks, staring at patterns for long periods of time, not making appropriate eye contact and resisting being held. Genie and I both taught at a medical school at the time and one day when Katie was about 6-months-old we literally ran into each other in the neuro-psychology section of the library stacks looking for clues. When she was not talking at age two we consulted a pediatric neurologist who declared that she had "autistic-like" features. We were left to continue our quest for a definitive diagnosis on our own. I sent away for "The Childhood Autism Rating Scale" developed by Dr. Eric Schopler of the TEACCH Program at the University of North Carolina. We had family and friends rate Katie on the scale and it was clear that Katie did have autism. This was later confirmed by the medical community when Katie was about 3 years old.

108

Now came the big challenge. As for all parents we did not know how were we to come to grip with this information. It felt like being told that your life and that of your family is going to be very different from now on. But there were no instructions on how to proceed. Strangely, there was a sense of relief to know at last what was wrong, even if it was what we had dreaded. There was also grief, a diffuse and deep sadness for Katie. This grief would reappear during the coming years, sometimes with even greater force. We began what would become a decade's long search to get Katie good services, including medical care, speech therapy and educational programs while simultaneously trying to figure out what the best services were, since the experts often did not seem to have much of a clue, especially at first. One nationally known expert on autism from the west coast met with Katie for an hour or so when she was around four years old and told us with total confidence that she would be going to a regular class room for first grade. A pediatric neurologist at a famous Midwestern hospital told us she would never be able to do anything for herself and may well end up in an institution. They were both wrong and Katie lives in a world somewhere in the middle.

Through this early period Katie was a great joy to us. She was beautiful, I say the most beautiful baby I ever saw, apologies to my other children. Little did we know that these baby years would be the best of times. As Katie got older and started "special education" we were in a constant struggle with the public school system and their complete lack of competence to deal with a child like Katie. There were a couple of years of relief when Katie had an excellent teacher who she still remembers and talks about. The problems magnified as Katie got older and I remember feeling guilty each day sending her off to what we knew would be a difficult day for her at school. She did survive with our frequent interventions and attempts to educate her teachers. We will never know how Katie would be today if she had been given a proper educational environment.

Katie was also the source of despair and depression to me as she went through a difficult adolescence. I became her focus of control over her world. She wanted me to sit in a certain chair, sometimes getting very upset if I did not have the exact posture she expected. She asked the same questions over and over and demanded that I respond in a specific way. As with many people with autism, familiar predictable response are a comfort. This was enough to make the most loving father nuts. I began to feel sorry for myself and felt in some sense my own life was over. My wife Genie would encourage me, but few other friends and family members understood the daily nature of our stress. We did not share the worse times with people. I think now that might have been a mistake, but the tendency was to protect our other children and elderly family members from worry.

Well, I did not die and I did not go off the deep end and mixed in with those bad times were times when Katie was the best thing in my life. She has a wonderful sense of humor. She loves to be silly and tell knock-knock jokes. She called her psychiatrist at a large teaching hospital, Mr. Big Tie. He took it with good grace and it never failed to tickle the teaching fellows that and accompanied him on our visits.

Katie is a music lover and when she would put on Fleetwood Mac and crank up the volume and dance, I would not want to be anywhere else on earth. She has taught me so many things about the world with her, at times, blunt honesty and unbiased observations. However, when expressed loudly in a public place these observations can be a tad embarrassing. I could claim that she has taught me patience, but she has some more work to do on that count.

In late in 2004, Katie was offered a spot in a group home near where we live. We had applied knowing that she had to have a permanent place as we grew older. But we feared the day the phone call would come. We told Katie that she was going to get her own apartment like her older brothers and sisters. She was not happy about this prospect and said she liked her home and wanted to stay with us. This conversation was during the Christmas holidays and she came down from her room after one of our discussions and pointing to the Christmas tree said, "I can't move. I've got presents under the tree." Our hearts just about broke on the spot.

But we knew there was no choice and that we faced the prospect of, as our family and friends put it, getting a life. Nonetheless, it was the most heart wrenching thing my wife and I ever did when we took her to her new home on that day in June. I am not sure anyone but the parent of a developmentally disabled child can understand this feeling. It is not like sending a child off to college, but more like sending your 6-year-old out into the world, even though the place we were sending her we knew was excellent.

We have her home frequently and I still have to sit in my chair sometimes if she is particularly anxious, but things are so much better for her and us. I no longer feel my "real" life is over. We enjoy simple things like taking a walk together or going out to dinner, none of which was possible for years without much preparation and worry.

It is hard to say what wisdom I would share with other fathers with children who are on the autism spectrum. If you do not have a sense of humor, especially about yourself, get one. As Katie tells me over and over, "Laughter is the best medicine." Get involved with other parents who have children with autism. I could have benefited from such contact when Katie was younger. Learning to share your feelings, even acknowledge them to yourself, is difficult for men. I would encourage any father to be open and seek help if you feel over stressed. Unfortunately many fathers leave the marriage because they think they can not handle their child's difficulties. I would urge anyone who had this cross their mind to recognize the tragedy it could mean for your child and spouse. I now get great comfort in sharing concerns and "Katie stories" with other parents. We all feel less alone when we are among others who understand what we are going through, both the joys and the sorrows.

Genie and I have begun an initiative with 60 other families in our area of North Carolina to build a residential community for adults on the autism spectrum using the best architectural and program practices available. We have been working on this project for about two years. If you would like more information contact me by phone our E-mail.

FAVORITE RESOURCES

Books: *Exiting Nirvana* by Clara Clairborne Clark/*Labeled Autistic* by Temple Grandin
Organizations: TEACCH UNC Chapel Hill, N. C. - Autism Society of America & NC

Russell, Daniel & Zachary

Illinois

Daniel, age 7 – Zachary, age 5
Daniel was diagnosed at 2½
Zachary was diagnosed at 2

CONTACT:
rluce721@yahoo.com

BIGGEST CHALLENGE(S)

To those fathers and mothers, or anybody else that reads these letters, I am Russell and a father of two sons that are autistic. Their names are Daniel (9) and Zachary(6). I am so happy to have this opportunity to express my feelings, my emotions, and the pride that I have in my kids. All parents face difficulties raising kids, but the challenges that we face with autism can be like trying to " drink water from a fire hose." Things are coming at you at a pace that can be overwhelming at times. To me, the unknown is probably the most upsetting and unnerving. As parents we would change places with our kids in a second but we can't. The day that we received the diagnosis of autism was upsetting and terrifying because I had limited knowledge of autism. As a father, the biggest challenges that I face are in learning more about autism and in making a positive impact in my boys' lives wherever and whenever I can .

GREATEST BLESSING(S)

When dealing with these challenges, sometimes I forget how much joy and happiness that my Daniel and Zachary bring to my life. I look at all of my children and see how beautiful they are (*I also have a child, Ronald, who does not have autism*). Yes, Daniel and Zachary face challenges every day, but they are happy. They smile and laugh. That laughter changes my day in a second when I hear it coming from them. It makes my day when they give me a smooch and hug, or they grab and hold my hand. I sometimes forget how special that is. I have a great relationship with my sons and I am so blessed for that. I want to say that I have great kids and that I will love them with all of my heart for the rest of my life .

WORDS OF WISDOM

We always need to remember that with every new day there is HOPE. I cannot emphasize that enough. Tomorrow may be the day that a great scientist or researcher gets us one step closer to helping our kids. I know that we will be there on the day we win the challenge of autism. The most important thing that I will say to those who will read this is keep the FAITH and keep facing each day with LOVE for your child (*or in our case children*). Thank you for reading this. If you would like to contact me please feel free at RLUCE721@yahoo.com.

Daniel, age 8, Russell, & Sundance (*Daniels's service dog*)

Russell & Timothy

Australia

Timothy, age 8
Timothy was diagnosed with Asperger's at 7

CONTACT:

rhansen@optusnet.com.au

Phone # (07) 3428 0007

My 8-year-old son, Timothy has Asperger's syndrome, with a healthy dose of Attention Deficit Hyperactive Disorder (ADHD) thrown in (*to keep things interesting*). It's a terrible combination. The ADHD makes it difficult to engage in any social activities, due to the inappropriate physical behavior; and the Asperger's makes it difficult in the same situations, for the inappropriate social etiquette behavior.

His 6-year-old brother, Joshua, suffers these same consequences, but he has yet to understand the full reasons why, and the pressure placed on him because of this is a lot for one so young.

As a result, we all spend a lot of time home together. From what I can see, this is not necessarily a bad thing. Their mum, my wife, Damaris, has always instilled a very expressive, open, and loving relationship between all of us. She has taught our boys, and me, each in our own ways, to say and show, how much we love and care for each other.

Joshua is a fantastic little boy who cares deeply about all things, and in some ways is having to mature quicker than a boy his age should. He's very understanding of Timothy's idiosyncrasies. Oh sure, they have regular bouts of sibling rivalry and the usual verbal jousts brothers have, but Joshua regularly shows his empathic side, when Timothy gets his way more often, and allowances are made for him that don't seem fair to most other kids.

Timothy on the other hand has a hard time showing his emotions in an extrovert manner. But my heart still melts when he's willing to stand up for his brother, if he perceives any injustice being done, or how he'll come and sit so his foot, shoulder, hand, etc., is touching you in some way, to show he cares.

My heart aches for Joshua when he draws the short end of the stick in family decisions, or when he just wants his brother's attention, but Timothy can't reciprocate. I ache just as much for Timothy when I see others look at him with no understanding at all, especially when he tries so hard to make friends and is either ridiculed or just plain rejected by those self-same kids.

But I feel sorry for many of those 'normal' families who are ships in the night, passing each other with barely any recognition. My family has it's fair share of bad days and heartache, but rather than let the waves of despair smash our ship to pieces, I keep sight on the blue skies and the horizon ahead, and know that while our journey may have it's ups and downs, I'm sailing with a fine crew, that no captain could ask more of.

Ryan & Evie

Indiana

Evie, age 3
Evie was diagnosed at 2 years

BIGGEST CHALLENGE(S)

I think the biggest challenge of being a father of an autistic child is relating to others how challenging and rewarding my child is. I feel very isolated because the general public views your child as either "normal," or just misbehaving, or stupid. The average person doesn't understand that most children with autism are very intelligent and bright and keep your life very interesting. You tend to feel very stuck in not being able to go out as a family and not having a normal life.

Autistic children often gravitate to their primary caregiver so as a father you feel left out. My daughter is so happy when her mother comes in the door and tends to ignore the fact when I or anyone such as her grandparents comes through the door. Evie tends to want her mother to do everything for her and she gets mad when I try to do it instead of her mother. So I have to learn not to take it personally.

We have found that finding funding for therapy is a challenge. I work for a national electronics and music retail store chain and their insurance doesn't cover autism treatment. They are self-funded insurance so they don't have to follow state mandates. The company says it has 'ethics and morals' in it's mission statement, but it is obvious that it does not. It feels as if my child's quality of life is not important to my employer. So this leaves us trying to get on government insurance, but we made too much by a couple hundred dollars a year. The fact was that the average cost of therapy was 75% of our yearly income. This is the tragedy of America's health care system. So we had to have my wife quit her part time job so we would qualify, thus leaving us living with no savings and barely able to pay bills. But my daughter gets the help she needs.

115

Greatest Blessing(s)

My greatest blessings are every time she laughs or makes me laugh. Evie often sings and dances around; given the chance to play dress up, she comes up with some interesting combos. She loves to build and play with blocks. Whenever she is at play or makes steps forward, that really touches my heart.

Words of Wisdom

As a father of an autistic child you often feel like your role in your child's life is not important, compared to the mothers, by therapists and doctors. I have found that a lot of fathers tend to withdraw from their child with autism. I make it a point to try to go to many of her appointments and to be involved as much as I can. Otherwise, I would miss the little things that make all the headaches worth it. Try to embrace your child and realize that your child with autism was put in your life for a reason, and that you can handle it.

Shawn & Khalen

Iowa

Khalen, age 3

Khalen was diagnosed at 2 years

CONTACT:
karabeauchamp@hotmail.com

BIGGEST CHALLENGE(S)

My biggest challenge is fighting a constant battle for a sense of normalcy. I see people who try and use his "disability" as an excuse to treat him differently. The problem is that he is too intelligent, observant and clever to be treated different. A few slurred words, and a bit of social uniqueness does not make him any different. All kids have their strengths and weaknesses, it's a universal truth. So I never treat him any different than any other kid. I know him better than most would at first impressions. He is funny, witty, and very smart. So when others finally see that it takes him one more step towards a world that understands; he's just like any other kid, full of great gifts and special faults. So how can one ever say he has a "disability"? …I know I can't.

Greatest Blessing(s)

Khalen. Not a creative answer, but simple questions get simple answers. You don't pick out certain things you like and don't like. You take him as he is, as a whole, or not at all.

Words of Wisdom

If you treat you child like they are 'different', instead of treating them like you treat everyone else, you might trick yourself into believing they are. All people are different, it's just a matter of whether you embrace others unique talents, or shun their individual flaws.

"The difference between a successful person and others is not a lack of strength, not a lack of knowledge, but rather in a lack of will."
– Vince Lombardi

Stanley & Peter

Pennsylvania

Peter was diagnosed
PDD/NOS at 4 years then
Aspergers with hypelexia

CONTACT:
Aspydad@comcast.net

BIGGEST CHALLENGE(S)

My son has many talents and abilities. He was fascinated by numbers and the alphabet before he could walk or talk (*he counted to 10 with his fingers*), and solved complex puzzles at 2 by sight, matching the pieces. He read spontaneously before he was 4 (*one of the enclosed pictures shows us reading together on the floor of his room before he was 1*), understood cursive writing before it was taught, and has tremendous rhythm and balance when he dances to music on his trampoline.

Others may not see these talents at first, if they can't look beyond his communications difficulties, and his obvious stims – and are amazed when we and his sister help him to show what he can do. Sometimes he seems to ignore others who try to speak to him, as if he prefers to live in a world of endless imaginary conversations with the fantasy friends he has created to take the place of the real ones he wants so badly, but just doesn't know how to make or sustain.

But when his immediate family members point out these abilities to others, or convince him to proudly show what he can do, they quickly realize how talented he is, far beyond their stereotype of a child with autism. We and his teachers are convinced that he can do great things, and one communications specialist in particular pushed for his inclusion in typical math class. There, his teacher quickly saw that he needed more challenge and stimulation than most of the rest of the class, and allowed him to try the advanced math game, 24, a year before typical peers would normally be exposed to it. They even have agreed with our belief that he should be evaluated for "gifted" programming, not withstanding his deficits in social skills and "pragmatics" (*the ability to hold a normal conversation*).

With all of these great attributes, what is my challenge then? I am afraid that the less desirable manifestations of his autism, that he struggles to control – the rage cycles, the anxiety over changes in routine and resulting behaviors – will keep him out of the good programs and discourage the great teachers who can help him develop those skills, and work with him on his behaviors. I want him to become the best version of himself (*to borrow a phrase from the inspirational speaker Matthew Kelly*). I am afraid each day that he won't get that chance, if those who can help him develop, don't even try, because of his most difficult moments.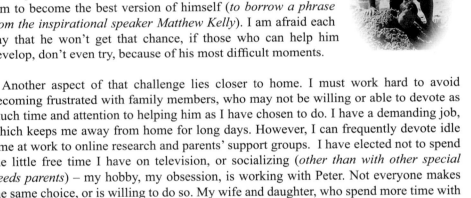

Another aspect of that challenge lies closer to home. I must work hard to avoid becoming frustrated with family members, who may not be willing or able to devote as much time and attention to helping him as I have chosen to do. I have a demanding job, which keeps me away from home for long days. However, I can frequently devote idle time at work to online research and parents' support groups. I have elected not to spend the little free time I have on television, or socializing (*other than with other special needs parents*) – my hobby, my obsession, is working with Peter. Not everyone makes the same choice, or is willing to do so. My wife and daughter, who spend more time with him during the week, each have their own active lives. I supported my wife's interest in learning to scuba dive when she needed a diversion from constantly dealing with the autism, and fortunately have the flexibility to work from home, or at nights, when she goes away. Peter's sister has all of the social savvy that her younger brother lacks, and has the ability to move among many different social circles – with athletes and artists alike – with ease.

So when I wish that I could sit and play chess with him or work through books on social skills that I ordered, but cannot because he has a different agenda for that day, I envy all the free time they have with him. In my mind, how could anyone not want to commit time to helping him improve? How could any family member not do all possible to help a child adrift in a world that he does not understand, and that all too often does not understand him?

So the challenge for me, then, is accepting that each of us in the family must come to our own terms with the autism. I know that each of us loves him unconditionally. Yet, I have also learned that each of us expresses that love in our own style, and not committing all the time that I do, doesn't mean they love him any less.

Instead, I am glad that my family lets me spend as much time at seminars or searching online as I need to satisfy my mission, just as I make the sacrifices to take care of Peter when they must go away for a break. I can't say that I have mastered this challenge yet, or that I don't become frustrated when they choose not to take him to an event that I might have done if I had not had work commitments. I am aware of why I get frustrated and can try to keep it from affecting our family life.

> "...autism has become such a fabric of our family life that I can no longer imagine a time when every decision, every event did not require us to plan around it"

GREATEST BLESSING(S)

Before my son's diagnosis, I was a typical middle class office worker, focused on advancing my career. Outside the office I had successfully raised funds for a local charity (*a legal clinic for the disabled*), I had begun supporting 5 years before Peter was born. Also, I was fortunate enough to have been solicited to join my parish's financial advisory council. Of course, I spent time with my wife and daughter on family activities (*when not preempted by the mother/daughter connection*).

After we began to understand Peter's struggles, I found a passion that I did not know that I had in me. Not only did I search for information and programs for our own use, but I also found how easy it had become to share my findings widely through the internet, with other parents and with teachers.

Although I had tried to be involved at my daughter's suburban elementary school, the reality of commuting to a center city job often made it difficult in the years before everyone had e-mail. Now, however, I can easily share information and observations with my son's teachers, and the parents of his classmates. We have been even more fortunate that he has had teachers who are willing to accept information and suggestions, and to correspond by e-mail when each of us has the time to do so. I have even been blessed to find support groups in which I could get involved, in my school district, and a local Asperger's group.

Now, I finally feel that I am leaving good works behind me, which I had never felt from years of writing contracts and legal news columns. I feel engaged with life in a way that I have not felt since I was an over-involved high school and college student. And I would not have found any of that without my son's diagnosis.

Certainly, I wouldn't suggest that anyone wish for a son on the spectrum as a bizarre way of finding fulfillment in life. That would treat my son as an object to my own end, rather than as a person deserving of attention for himself.

But we have to live the one life we have, without regrets for what might have been. I am thankful that I had the energy, the supportive family, and the faith in God to find a positive response to my son's diagnosis to help him. To my surprise, in trying to help him I found that I helped myself at the same time.

WORDS OF WISDOM

When my son was younger, I spent many weekends playing whatever he wanted, however repetitive or illogical it may have seemed at the time. In Peter's case, that was a search for *Blue's Clues* – always the same clues, in the same locations, always leading to the same answer to the same question.

But by following his lead, I came to appreciate the special privilege Peter had granted me. By living in his world, however briefly, I went on vacation to an exclusive resort. "Peter's world" was open only for a few short years, never to be seen again. But to get in and enjoy it, I had to share that precious, brief time there together with him. If I had to play the same game with him, again and again, that was just the price of admission to the resort. I was glad to pay it, and consider it cheap for the joy it gave me.

I will never again visit the world of four-year-old Peter. But I remember it fondly, for the times we shared together – far better than I recall the therapy sessions, or tantrums. Now, I instead visit the world of an eight year old, inhabited by characters from different television shows, and, to my delight, from stories he created in his own rich imagination. Although that world will also close all too soon, I know that adventures in the worlds of nine and ten year old Peter await me, with all their pleasures to be discovered. Occasionally, we smile together when we glimpse a dog named Blue, which brings warm memories to both of us.

As Dads, we only get a brief visit from a little boy, who won't wait for us while we dally with the autism. Let's be certain we enjoy that all too short time together with our boys, wherever they want to take us.

Shortly after my son's diagnosis in December, 2001, he lay awake, miserable from an infection, and unable to sleep. He didn't yet have the words to tell us what was bothering him, and certainly couldn't understand why he felt so badly. To calm him, I lay next to him in bed, rubbing his back for comfort and security. I was whispering familiar, calming phrases to him, to try to take his mind off his discomfort.

Although I was trying to calm him, I needed peace as well. As I lay with him, free of the day-to-day concerns of work and holiday planning, my own mind raced with worries about the future, for both him and our family. I hadn't yet started to read about the therapeutic options available, or even about the many different places on the "autism spectrum". Instead, I multiplied his misery with my own growing despair, about developmental "delays" we didn't yet understand. I tried to understand the nuances of autism and PDD and Asperger's, and which was "better." In my ignorance, the diagnosis seemed to close a book on our family's and Peter's life, that hadn't even been written yet.

In the hope that I could relax Peter enough to sleep, I kept reassuring him that I, and the rest of our extended family, loved him. Maybe I needed to convince myself as much as him. But as I spoke, comforting words naturally flowed out of my mouth, unbidden. "Peter, Daddy loves you just the way you are, and Mommy loves you just the way you are, and your sister loves you just the way you are. And God Who made you loves you just the way you are. If you're good enough for Jesus, how can you not be good enough for me?"

I was stunned by how obvious their wisdom appeared at that moment. My own fears had blinded me to the reality that "my little boy with autism" was still "my little boy" just the same. Certainly, no one can deny that raising an autistic child is difficult at times. Every daily task, no matter how small, can be challenging.

The stress seems like it never stops, from problem behaviors at home and in church or at neighbors' houses, to battles over school placements, and the search for friends to play with. Even taking a walk with your spouse becomes difficult, when siblings or relatives may not yet be comfortable watching him. Vacations present an overwhelming change from routine. Yet that night, I realized the best gift I can give to my son. Like any child, diagnosis or not, he just needs unconditional love. Although tantrums, rigidity, and unresponsiveness make this basic act of parenthood more difficult, he needs it all the more. Perhaps I didn't realize who really needed comfort more that night, my fidgeting son or me. Fortunately, I found the strength to remain by his side, that night and beyond.

Now, when he is at his most challenging, I recall that simple phrase that popped into my head that night: *"God, Who made you, loves you just the way you are. If you're good enough for Jesus, how can you not be good enough for me?"* With the peace I gained from that understanding, I know that I cannot, and will not, allow any behavior, no matter how challenging, to interfere with my love for him.

Autism is a thief. It has stolen not only the life with my son that I imagined and expected when he was born, but also the family life that we once had – along with my memories of that time.

Peter's sister will graduate from high school this year, when Peter is eight. She is fortunate to have an aunt who has assembled a collection of pictures of her life. At a family graduation party, she was thrilled to receive the book as a graduation present. Yet, as I paged through memories of her life, I was shocked at how little I remembered of the times we spent together when she was younger, before Peter was born, and when he was young and we didn't understand why his behavior was difficult. Certainly, I was in the pictures, but I don't have a current recall of those times, happy as they were with our daughter.

Sadly, I think that autism has become such a fabric of our family life that I can no longer imagine a time when every decision, every event did not require us to plan around it. I no longer think of birthday parties, family gatherings or school concerts as something to which we go as a family. Instead, everything has become, "Who will go, and who will stay with Peter?" Not only has the autism consumed our lives today, but for me, at least, it has also robbed me of the ability to recall what life was like before our son was born. Fortunately, pictures exist to remind us of that time, when the autism was not the prism through which all else passed. Hopefully our daughter has her own happy memories, which are not as tinged as my own with regret for a life that has been lost, that might have been lived more fully and joyfully.

I can't deny that I have had many happy times with my son, for which I have fond memories. Looking through the images of my daughter's life, I realize how much autism has consumed all of our thoughts, even when Peter was not involved. I enjoyed those times as they happened, but in retrospect, remember only the struggles of dealing with the day-to-day problems caused by the autism.

I encourage fathers starting down the road to make the effort, hard as it may be, to carve out the time to live a full life with your other children, and with your spouse. If you do not, you could wake up one day, like me, without memories of a life without it.

"How wonderful it is that nobody need wait a single moment before starting to improve the world"

— Anne Frank

"Since you cannot do good to all, you are to pay special attention to those who, by the accidents of time, or place, or circumstances, are brought into closer connection with you"

— St. Augustine of Hippo

Steve & Craig

Michigan

Craig was diagnosed at
3 years

BIGGEST CHALLENGE(S)

I think one of the biggest challenges for me, having a child with autism, was the change of my dreams for my son that came with the diagnosis. I remember thinking, 'What kind of life will he have?' as I heard all of the things the doctor told us he would never achieve. I have dreams for both of my children just as all fathers do, and will do whatever I can to see my dreams and their own dreams come true. Jacob, my neuro-typical 8-year-old, will tell you that he will play football for a professional team. I can see this dream of his and how it fits with my dreams of independence and happiness for him. This was an easy dream for me to have for him, but for Craig, my 6-year-old son with autism, it was much harder. I remember asking him one day, "What do you want to do when you are big?" I really didn't expect much of an answer. He surprised me when he looked at me with his big eyes and lopsided grin and said, "I want to play basketball". This was the point for me when I realized I could have dreams for him and I just needed to realign them with his. I wanted him to be independent and happy but it might not look the same as I thought it should. This is also when I started to think about how I had allowed the "professional's" limitations and stipulations to guide my thinking. I had heard so many of the, 'he won't be able to's' and 'he won't ever's', and I allowed those to set up barriers in my mind of what he can do.

GREATEST BLESSING(S)

This being said, I now never underestimate what Craig can do. Despite all of his sensory issues, lack of motor planning skills, and fine motor delays he is still so much a typical 6-year-old boy. Last summer when he rode his bike for the first time (*one of those things they said he would never do*) it brought tears of joy to my eyes and excitement to see what he would do next. Now he never ceases to amaze me. He played on a tee ball team this year for the first time, and he is jumping into water over his head and swimming with friends at the pool. He is all smiles and laughter and works hard to make friends. I wonder if all the "professionals" that gave us all the limitations could see him now would rethink their telling families what their children won't do or achieve.

I think the thing that bothers me the most is the sympathy you get from people when they learn you have a child with autism. I get the usual "*OH, I am so sorry*", or "*that must be so hard on you*". I used to just look at people not sure what to say, but now I am a little more vocal. I tell them that I consider my son a blessing and there is not a day that goes by that he does not brighten my day, add a smile my to face, or laughter to my heart. I am not saying that there are not trying times too, the constant ripping of paper, the late nights being woken up when he helps himself to a snack, or the tantrums when he does not get his way or the ones that we have no idea what caused them. (*I secretly think that he gets this from his mom*). We constantly are watching what we say for fear he will repeat it. When these things start to wear on me, I remind myself that without these trying times the sweetness of the good times would not be as sweet.

I get asked sometimes if I wish he were "normal". I think about this and wonder just what is normal? If normal means not having to fight for services for him, or having to run to all sorts of therapy appointments, or go to endless IEP's, then yes, I wish he was normal. But if normal means I have to give up watching him react so naturally to his surroundings, then I do not wish it all. All the hard things are worth it just to watch Craig fully enjoy his life and the everyday things we take for granted. It is priceless to see the joy on his face as he walks through the grass barefoot, stopping to rub the grass all over him just because it feels good, or splashing around a mud puddle and then dipping his head into it because it looks like fun. I envy how he does not worry about what other's think and is uninhibited when it comes to enjoying what the world has to offer. I think the world would be a better place if we all could adopt this philosophy and care-free attitude.

> "We constantly are watching what we say for fear he will repeat it"

WORDS OF WISDOM

If I had any words of wisdom for other fathers they would be to not forget your dreams, they don't have to go away, you just might have to rearrange them. Also, make sure that teaching them independence is still part of that dream. Second is to have great expectations for your child. The moment you lower expectations then your child will meet those expectations and they may have more to achieve but might not have the chance. The third is the most important, and that is to enjoy your child no matter how challenging your child maybe, always remember to savor every little positive.

Steven & Nathan

Nebraska

Nathan, age 11
Nathan was diagnosed at 5

BIGGEST CHALLENGE(S)

We've had many challenges over the years regarding tactile issues, communication issues, and social issues. The biggest challenge we face now is teaching Nathan social skills. Personal space, personal hygiene, conversational skills, and appropriate public behavior are issues that concern me the most at this time. As peer pressure is not a factor, many situations that a non-autistic child would learn simply by observation are lost on Nathan. We are working closely with his school, as well as with a local program for special needs children, to help Nathan overcome some of these challenges.

I personally work with my own challenges regarding my son. The feelings of guilt and fear. The guilt manifests itself in questions to myself. Is it my fault that Nathan is autistic? Could I have done something to prevent it? Could I have done more over the years to help my son? Rationally, I know the answers to those questions, but the guilt remains. The fear is more concrete. I fear what will happen to Nathan if something were to happen to me. Even if I were to live a long life, there will still come a time when I will no longer be able to care for him. It scares me to think of Nathan as an older man without me there to advocate for him.

GREATEST BLESSING(S)

My greatest blessing, aside from Nathan himself and the joy he brings me, is the fact that he can carry a conversation with me. For many years Nathan was unable to speak. When we realized that there was a good chance he might not ever speak we started teaching Nathan simple sign language skills. The school was very helpful and coordinated their teaching to improve Nathan's sign language skills. The summer after Nathan's sixth birthday was very special. One day he was playing a Mario Brothers video game and said the word "Mario." I couldn't believe it. I asked him to say it again and he did. His speech skills improved rapidly after that. Today, when Nathan looks up at me and says that he loves me, I think back to a time when he couldn't. It's very special to me and I never take it for granted.

> "It scares me to think of Nathan as an older man without me there to advocate for him"

WORDS OF WISDOM

One of the most important things I've learned as I've grown with Nathan is to always keep an open mind. In order for me to try and understand some of the frustrations and joys that Nathan experiences, I must first throw out my preconceived thoughts and ideas. I must continuously reassess my perception of daily life events and open my mind to the fact that Nathan's perception of these same events does not match my own. As an example, when Nathan was two-years-old he required that upon entering the home the lights be turned on in a specific sequence. To allow a non-autistic child his wish in this could certainly be perceived as spoiling the child. However, in Nathan's case it was extremely discomforting to him to the point of almost physical pain. It takes an open mind to stop and think what a simple task such as this may mean to Nathan. It also takes a good understanding of your child to recognize the difference between, "I want my way" and "This makes me extremely uncomfortable." Unconditional love, compassion, and a solid attempt at empathy will go a long way in achieving this.

Organizations:
Heartland Equine Therapeutic Riding Academy / www.hetra.org
Munroe-Meyer Institute for Genetics and Rehabilitation / www.unmc.edu/mmi/

Todd & Brandon

Texas

Brandon was diagnosed at 18 months

CONTACT:
TGuppy@LGC.com
www.TexasAutismAdvocacy.org

BIGGEST CHALLENGE(S)

As this Father's Day approaches I have been thinking about what it means to be a father and also what it means to be the father of a "special needs" child. Initially, Father's Day was a day I would look forward to getting the latest power tool to work around the house. I love to build things out of wood and have always enjoyed working in my garage/ woodshop with the boys. My first-born son, Matthew and I, love to construct things from wood; being only limited by our imagination. Brandon my "special boy" just loves to be with us and around all the buzzing and spinning power tools.

I always feel a bit closer to Jesus when I am wood-working, knowing that I am shaping wood to be used and enjoyed for years to come, just as He did in His day. (*Except for the cool power tools, of course.*)

This year is different as I have had time to reflect and examine some things I have experienced since last Father's Day.....

In the last year we have experienced some difficult times concerning Brandon. Any day with autism can be a challenge, but the real challenges started when I was in the garage on a Saturday morning working. Brandon and I were the only ones home. Brandon had just gone in the house, most likely for a drink. I heard a thump. I went to investigate and found Brandon lying on the floor kind of jerking around. I carried his jerking body to the couch to try to figure out was wrong. Our house is locked down tighter than Fort Knox, so I couldn't imagine anything he could have gotten into. Did he swallow something? Some object or some chemical? What does he need? What do I do? As a man who has the tools and the knowledge, (*if not just sheer determination in some cases*) to fix just about anything — I found myself helpless.

Now he was shaking more violently and still unaware — 911? The phone is in the next room and he would fall on the floor if I left him. So I stayed there with him and prayed as I never had before. He began to settle and become somewhat aware of me. At some point I realized I was crying and just thankful to God that Brandon was okay. Since Brandon seemed okay, I was okay.

We soon found out that Brandon had started having seizures. This had never happened before and we were set-back a step or two, but we still had it all together. I explained what happened to Michelle (*my wife*) and Matthew (*my older son*) in case it happened again. Of course it did happen again and this time I was not home and my explanation did not prepare them for what they saw. The ambulance was soon on the way, Brandon had another Grand Mal, but he was okay. A broken collar bone from it, but okay.

The doctors assured us that the medication would control the seizures. God had another plan. Brandon was not only having Grand Mal seizures but was now also having Atonic (*drop*) seizures. As I quickly learned, the Grand Mal were more involved, but the drop seizures were more devastating and physically dangerous. I was now just borderline okay.

Now, Brandon was having 10 or more of the drop seizures a day. We learned to do nearly everything while holding Brandon's hand and never letting him be out of our reach. He would be sitting having breakfast, just totally go limp and smack his head on the table on the way to the floor. Then, immediately, he would be fully aware again, bleeding and crying with a huge bump on his head and cheerios dripping from the wall.

We ordered a helmet for him to protect his face and head, but it didn't arrive soon enough. He cut his eyebrow open during a fall and it was another trip to the emergency room. I went to work and when I came back that evening he dropped to the floor and shattered his teeth. I was no longer okay. He was laying there having a seizure and bleeding everywhere, and missing one permanent front tooth, and parts of 3 other teeth.

I was NOT okay.

I was at the end of the rope, and so was Michelle. We were seriously unable to cope at that point. We were both so distraught that we were of no use to each other. I wanted to start punching walls and not stop – and Michelle could not stop sobbing over and over, "I cannot believe God let that happen." So we called the Pastor. He arrived within minutes, "Why," we asked him. We have been praying for the safety of our son and yet harm happened to him anyway. Why? We knew God heard our prayers, but why didn't He answer them? We were NOT okay with that!! Bryan, along with our very comforting next door neighbors began to calm us down by simply assuring us that God was still God and perhaps He wasn't done with us yet.

Brandon survived the dental surgery. He wore his helmet every minute he was awake and finally we began to feel more at ease. His whole room was void of anything sharp and our kitchen floor and his bedroom floor was covered with wall to wall padding, thanks to Denise and the Joy Ministry.

Then we were all out back testing out a new above ground pool (*thanks to Thad and Denise*). Brandon had been swimming and just started climbing up the 4 foot ladder to get out. He stepped to the landing on the top and as I was moving across the pool to grab him to get him down, he had a seizure, went limp, and fell backwards head first down 4 feet to the concrete with no arms out to catch him from the fall. I leapt over the side of the pool expecting to find a very different site than what I found. He was okay except for a scrape on the side of his head.

We knew the force of a Drop seizure from sitting in a chair and knew that a Drop seizure from the top of that ladder to concrete was most certainly a very bad scenario. But nothing had happened, and in fact, Brandon did not even cry. I kept saying … 'It is NOT possible. It is NOT possible.' Guess what. It is possible because God was in control. I began to trust God as never before, as there was no other explanation for what had happened. God was obviously not done with Brandon, or with me.

One evening, Brandon was playing in the back yard under very tight surveillance. I had gone inside for a moment. Michelle walked by the window to check on Brandon and saw him lying flat on the grass, not moving, with the sprinkler spraying up and landing on his chest and face. As Brandon's mother, she knew something was very wrong. So wrong that she screamed for me to go get him because she couldn't bear to. I carried his cold, limp, and unresponsive body to the house. I was assuming it was too late. No seizure activity. No movement at all. I checked his pulse. None that I could find. I used to work in the emergency room so finding a pulse was not new to me. I could not hear any breathing or see any chest movement. I started mouth-to-mouth as Michelle called 911 – yet again.

Since this was a call for a child that had quit breathing, the first of several trucks showed up within 2 minutes. It was like they dropped out of the sky. In that time, I finally heard the slightest of breaths from Brandon but he was still unresponsive. Not shaking this time, just limp.

Our theory was that Brandon, who loves water and loves to catch it in his mouth from the sprinkler, had been doing that when a seizure hit and he swallowed enough water to cause him to choke and stop breathing. No matter the explanation, he was okay, and so was I.

During this whole process I had been taken to the depths of doubt and disappointment about God and his protection and care over my family. It was hard to believe what God said in the *Bible* about always being there. I guess though, I started believing when Brandon fell backwards from the ladder. I totally believed when God took Brandon from us for what seemed like eternity after finding him in the backyard unconscious. That is when I finally got it.

Although the road had always been tough, it took those 'seizure' trials for me to get the point of trusting God in a way that I never could have imagined or attained without them. Through those trials God was there. Even when I felt He wasn't. He sent the church members to feed us when we needed it. He sent friends to comfort us when we were down. He sent Bryan to encourage and remind us of His promises, when we questioned. Most of all, he caught Brandon when he fell from the ladder that should have cracked his skull and brought him back after we thought it was too late.

He had always provided. The most unexplainable thing of all, is that Brandon is off all his medication and has not had any type of seizure since December. We had scheduled a certain kind of surgery to implant a device that would hopefully control the seizures, as the four medications we had tried were not working. Surgery was our only option left. Then, with no warning, the seizures stopped. The doctors could not explain it. But I can. God was always there for us and he is there for you too. Reach out and trust him. We are his children, he is our heavenly Father.

I don't know what challenges lie ahead for us in the future, but for now I do know that I have learned how to give up control and trust God to watch over my son. This Father's Day I am just so thankful for the little things... Brandon and his wonderful smile and laughter. His giggles as he runs away so I'll catch him and wrestle him — that totally lights up my world and makes it all worthwhile.

I thank you, my Heavenly Father, for both of my children; and especially Brandon, as he has changed my life and my outlook forever.

Amen.

> "I do know that I have learned how to give up control and trust God to watch over my son"

Todd & Brian

Illinois

Brian was diagnosed PDD/NOS at 27 months

BIGGEST CHALLENGE(S)

The challenges of raising Brian range from managing life-altering thoughts to the more mundane frustrations of everyday life with a child on the [autism] spectrum.

On the life-altering side, the biggest challenge has been to scale back some of the hopes, dreams, and expectations that all parents inherently have for their kids without even thinking about it. For example, before having Brian, I had visions of a child in college, a child getting married, and a child living independently. Since Brian's diagnosis, we as a family have learned so much more about the challenges that adults on the spectrum face. Without even thinking about the next few years, my mind immediately races ahead to 'will Brian ever have a loving, committed relationship with another adult?' 'Will Brian go to college?' 'Will Brian be able to hold down a job?' Having to answer these questions with a resounding "maybe" is a tremendous challenge that most parents have the luxury of not having to face. It is a challenge I was not prepared for, and it threatens the whole core of what I thought being a parent would be. I have had to reshape my dreams for Brian 'just in case' he faces life-long challenges. I still have dreams for Brian, but I am very cautious in my thoughts so as not to be disappointed for him or in him.

Another major challenge is the isolation we feel from friends and family who either don't understand the complexity of dealing with Brian's situation, choose to ignore or minimize Brian's challenges, or make us feel pitiful for the challenges we face. It is very difficult to converse with parents of neuro-typical children. For one thing, their stories of what their children say or do shed light on things that Brian does not or cannot do. In addition, their worries (*e.g., will their child be able to attend pre-school with his or her friends*) seem so petty while we are faced with questions like will Brian be able to live independently. I am not by any means a bitter person, but social interactions with adults who have not gone through what we have, challenge my patience.

On the mundane side, there are many everyday challenges such as getting Brian's full attention, which would come so naturally for other kids. There are also the challenges of managing Brian's OCD-type behaviors (*e.g., getting him to go potty without first playing with the toilet seat or getting him to walk by a certain landmark without saying the same thing*). These quirks make Brian who he is and they are so very endearing, but they create a constant pressure to urge Brian to "do things a different way."

GREATEST BLESSING(S)

The greatest blessing of having a child on the spectrum is the depth with which it forces you to understand your child. Brian won't always tell me how he's feeling or what's making him anxious. Therefore, the burden is on me to get in tuned with him. I feel so overwhelmingly connected to Brian because I feel that the only way to truly understand him is to get right in there with him and try to feel what he's feeling. There is no such thing as going through the motions with Brian. Each interaction I have with him involves me trying to get inside his head to make sure I am giving him what he needs, even if he cannot always express it.

Another great blessing in disguise is the way in which facing certain challenges strips away some of the BS that parents often get bogged down in. Do I care of Brian ever wins a popularity contest at school? Do I give a rat's a*s where his next birthday party is? Not anymore I don't. I simply want him to live a happy, peaceful, not-so-anxious independent life that involves close relationships with his family and maybe a few friends. Boy what a difference a few years makes in tailoring these dreams for him. Part of this process (*stripping away certain dreams*) is profoundly sad. However, deep down I see it as a blessing to focus on what's really important in life – the happiness of one's child – while putting to one side some of the things society tells parents they should be consumed with.

Words of Wisdom

- Have date nights with your spouse or partner. A happy marriage is essential to maintaining mental health. Kids on the spectrum need you both.

- When possible, don't judge your kid. It's not his or her fault that they can't do things that other kids can do. They're just different, not inferior.

- Don't stop dreaming for your child. Just dream "outside the box."

- Don't let anyone tell you "nothing's wrong" if you know something is.

- Meet your child where he or she is. Anybody who says you can't watch the same episode of *The Wiggles* four times in a row doesn't have a kid on the spectrum.

- Appreciate the idiosyncrasies of your child. I'm sure you have some, too.

- Educate your family. Kids on the spectrum need continuity so it's nice when everyone's on the same page for how to interact with the child.

- Don't force your kid to fit into the plans you had for them (*if your son doesn't love sports, go find a rec league team for yourself*).

- Seek early, intense intervention. Kids on the spectrum can improve or be cured.

- Keep fighting for additional research for a cure. This issue is far too under the radar.

- Don't listen to me (*I'm no expert*) – follow your own heart.

Favorite Resources

www.nationalautismassociation.org
www.tacanow.org
www.generationrescue.org
www.autism.com/ari
www.rdiconnect.com

Tony & Frankie

Illinois

Frankie, age 7
Frankie was diagnosed at just over 16 months

CONTACT:
tonyfalco2002@yahoo.com

BIGGEST CHALLENGE(S)

The biggest challenge I face with Frankie is getting educational services that address his needs and are engaging and challenging. As we have learned, systems and schools are very different. We had to move from a neighborhood with friends that loved, understood, and even looked out for Frankie to an unknown neighborhood all because the school district was more stable and better equipped to help Frankie now and as he gets older. I don't know how to convey to you the feelings we had. Is this the right thing to do? Will the transition out of the only house he's known be worse than leaving him in a less than equipped school system? Am I sacrificing my younger son's happiness for his brother's? This was not only the hardest decision to make, it was also one of the most important. After months of worrying how Frankie would transition with this monumental change in his life, he seemed to adjust the easiest. Not bad for a boy that only a few years before would tantrum and bang his head if you took a different route to school or Wendy's!

As Frankie gets older it is harder to find dependable and capable respite workers. This constant scrutinizing of our schedules so that one of us is always home is extremely exhausting. We do go out with the entire family but we can do that only in a few select places. Family parties are tiresome also, unless they are at our house. As the years go on, it is virtually impossible to go to friend's houses. Most of our friends and family know that if they want to carry on at least one conversation with us then our get-together should be planned at our house. Our freedom of doing even the simplest tasks takes careful thought and planning. Over the years it can wear you down to where you don't even want to think about going out, alone or with the kids. On the occasion we would get some respite and have a night out, many times our night out would end with hearing such terrible reports from the sitter that it makes you think twice before going out again. I LOVE MY SON WITH EVERY FIBER OF MY SOUL BUT I DESPISE AUTISM EVEN MORE!

Another challenge I confront is making sure I compensate for our restricted lives by spending quality time with my younger son. He can't typically play with Frankie so I've tried to be not only his Dad but also his playmate. There aren't many kids on our new block so Dad would jump on the trampoline with him as he complains, "I'm bored, Dad, can you play with me?" Don't get me wrong, I really love it and we have a great relationship but it's just another piece to balance on my plate, another thing to think and worry about.

I also worry about Frankie's future. What will happen to him when my wife and I are not around to care for him? Can I provide for him to live as I want him to live? The thought of Frankie not properly cared for and nobody checking to see that he's being treated properly makes both me and my wife sick to our stomachs. We need to appoint a guardian in case something happens to us. Who should it be? Can they do it? Will they do it? Do they have any idea how this will impact their lives? As a father of a son with autism, I have many questions. I pray that soon I will also have the right answers.

GREATEST BLESSING(S)

Being Frankie's dad has brought me many blessings. I believe it has made me a better father to both of my boys. No accomplishment is small. I look at everything differently. I work harder at being a dad than I might if Frankie weren't autistic. When he was younger I can't tell you how many hours we spent with me pushing him on our backyard swing, and I liked it. Being with him, playing with him, tucking him in bed at night did more for me than it ever did for him. He's taught me far more than any son can teach a father. As I look into those beautiful baby blues I would see this ecstatic little boy looking back at me and saying,

"Isn't this great, Dad?" My son is non-verbal but we have had many meaningful conversations. You would think that I would do most of the talking but actually it was I who did most of the listening.

I believe these times we've spent together have benefited my younger son also. I try and spend quality time alone with him and rarely say 'no' if he asks me to do something with him. This blessing from Frankie has enriched me as a father more than I could imagine.

WORDS OF WISDOM

What mind-set I believe helps me the most is, "Take one day at a time." The entire journey may seem less daunting if looked at step-by-step. It is a bit ironic but this is exactly what helps Frankie grasp things at school, they break up an entire process into small parts and then put them all together to achieve the desired goal. Here we go again — son teaching dad!

Don't ever say, "It can't get any worse," or that, "God doesn't give you more than you can handle" to a father of an autistic child. Never!

Finally, I always try to remember the suggestion of a poem that my wife found about a couple about to have a baby and the baby is born with special needs. It's like planning your dream vacation to go to Italy. It says how you plan for months, reading up on all Italy has to offer, very excited about all you are going to experience. Unexpectedly, your plane is forced to land in Holland and there you must stay. It isn't a horrible place, just different. They must go back and re-plan their trip. They meet a whole different group of people that they probably would never have met. It's slower-paced but after awhile you notice that Holland has windmills, and tulips, and even Rembrandts. Everyone you know is busy coming and going from Italy and bragging about their wonderful time. You planned that trip. That pain of losing that dream will never go away. But if you spend your life mourning that you didn't get to Italy, you may never enjoy the very special, very lovely things about Holland. Enjoy the trip as best you can.

*Editor's note: The story Tony refers to is **Welcome to Holland** by Emily P. Kinsley*

Tony & Shawn

Maine

Shawn was diagnosed at 2

CONTACT:
egyptsas2@hotmail.com

BIGGEST CHALLENGE(S)

Our biggest challenge with Shawn is trying to understand what he needs. For the most part, he is non-verbal. So trying to figure out what he wants and needs, where he hurts, why he is crying, or why he is physically hurting himself or us. My biggest fear of all is what will happen to Shawn in the future. Will he be able to care for himself even partially, could my wife do this alone if something happened to me, and will his needs be so demanding after he gets older?

Greatest Blessing(s)

My greatest blessing is my wife, Anite, and the love she has to give. The patience and determination she gives Shawn in fighting for him no matter what it takes, and we know it takes a lot.

"The little things means so much"

Words of Wisdom

Have patience, love and understanding.

Patience
for all you will have to endure.

Love
for your family, what you feel down deep in your soul, and what you get back; the little things mean so much.

Understanding
for others: what they are feeling, going through, sacrificing. Emotions can seem magnified when you are going through rough times, I think because the duration of everything, so try to stay understanding.

Favorite Resource

gfcfkids@yahoo.com

Travis & Kiara

Arkansas

Kiara, age 6
Kiara was diagnosed at 2

CONTACT:
travispeggydurham@yahoo.com

BIGGEST CHALLENGE(S)

My name is Travis, I am a father of a 7-year-old who has Pervasive Development Disorder/Not Otherwise Specified (*PDD-NOS*). It is a daily struggle sometimes not understanding everything there is to know about autism. I have run from doctor to doctor with my wife and our daughter. I have spent many nights and days rubbing my head being frustrated because I feel like we get somewhere and Kiara is progressing and then out of nowhere, she'll relapse, or some type of a 'new' behavior starts to show. I have seen my wife cry from being so frustrated, not knowing what to do. I have sat with my daughter and tried to explain to her the best way that I know how, that she is normal to us, even if other's may not think so.

Kiara struggles in school with her writing skills and her comprehension. We have fought and fought with the schools to get the extra help for her that she needs and they have told us that she does fine. Don't get me wrong, she's very smart!

141

She has a great long-term memory, but her short-term memory doesn't seem to be all that great. We are seeing where she's having problems and just want the schools to help where they need to. Kiara is currently in Speech and Occupational Therapy. She has been in speech since the age of 3.

Kiara also has been recently diagnosed with Pati Mal seizures and some doctors think that she might have Partial Seizures on top of that. She also has tics. Not the full blown Tourette's syndrome, but the tics of it. All this for a 7-year-old child, and I think to myself, 'Why my daughter?'

I see the way people look at my daughter and I get mad. Physically, she looks normal, but when she has a meltdown, you can see them staring and talking. Why can't they understand it's not her fault? It is not because of bad parenting. This is just as hard for her and our family as it is for them to see it. Some of her meltdowns have been severe. We have had to have her doctor write a note stating her diagnosis and that's why she acts the way she does.

GREATEST BLESSING(S)

Being a father of a child with autism is very challenging as you have read, but there are also blessings that come with it too.

When you see that your child is progressing and learning new ways to cope and deal, or just learning new things, you think to yourself, 'Wow, she couldn't do this two days ago,' and it is GREAT to see this.

I remember when Kiara was 3 and 4-years-old, she wouldn't let anyone touch her, period! No hugs and no kisses. You can only imagine what that's like until you have experienced this yourself. Now, here at the age of 7, she tells me, "I love you daddy," with a hug and a kiss. That's a blessing!

WORDS OF WISDOM

The only thing that I can tell other fathers and/or other parents is — be patient, keep them in whatever therapies you have to. It really pays off when your child comes to you. It may not happen all the time, but the first time that they do and they tell you what it is that they want and can point at it all at the same time, it's just a great feeling!

"I have seen my wife cry from being so frustrated, not knowing what to do"

William, Billy & Mark

Virginia

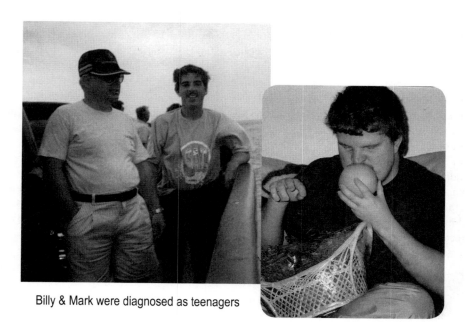

Billy & Mark were diagnosed as teenagers

CONTACT:

conky4you@wmconnect.com
540-433-0715

My wife and I are the parents of two adult sons with autism and severe mental retardation. Billy is 37, and Mark is 32, and blind. My wife had rubella when she carried Mark. Mark is an echolalia savant. He even mocks Spanish language when he chooses. Both are on many drugs to alleviate their symptoms. In middle age, Billy has developed asthma and incontinence; therefore has a low stamina for the sports he once enjoyed. Mark has dystonia and does not desire to swim or walk in the parks anymore. He prefers to listen to TV and books in his own room. Billy and I take our dog, Cece, for a truck ride every Saturday and then get a pop. Their mom takes them to watch horses and buggies going to church on Sundays, while eating breakfast they get in a drive-thru. We take turns going to church. We tried taking them for many years, but had to stop, because Mark could not handle the noises. Billy is more social and my wife takes him to the mall every week for pizza, but he bops her on the head, steps on her feet and pulls on her, so no one can talk to her.

Biggest Challenge(s)

Finding services so our boys can get along in life is our biggest challenge. Also, it is mandated by law, we should have respite. I am now retired and would still like to take my wife alone on a vacation. We can't because there is no respite for us.

School for both our sons was a nightmare because professionals did not understand why they had behaviors which escalated into aggressions and destruction of property. We could handle them when they were smaller, but when they reached their teens and they got bigger and stronger, was when our real difficulties began. They react to situations in life and very little behavior intervention helps. Billy carries yellow nerf balls in his hands and pants pockets and looks big and lumpy (*try dealing with this in public, ha*). We worry, knowing in the future with our ages, our sons will have to go to a group home and we wonder if they will make it because of their difficulties with noise, stimuli, and changes. It is bad enough having kids you can't work with, and often times it feels as if no one in our state seems to want to work with them either. We have no services in this community.

Professionals should have empathy and work harder to get families support; and a knowledge of autism would be a plus! More public awareness would be great. Even other families who have a retarded child do not understand ours and wonder why we don't make them listen. We have given our sons every opportunity in life to excel when they can.

Greatest Blessing(s)

Our greatest blessing was getting an aide for Billy in school when he was suspended. We are grateful for their day programs from 9-2, which provides us our only break. I am glad that we are still able to take care of our sons and we can relate to all minority groups and their problems in this world. I am, therefore, humbled.

Our main support has been other parents who have the same problem. Mark having his own small apartment in our home has helped both sons be able to tolerate each other. They love each other but just for little spurts at a time. (*ha*)

Words of Wisdom

When your kids can't change, you must. Be prepared to fight the system and do all you can to get what your kids need. Do the best you can with what you have.

> "What do we live for if not to make life less difficult for each other?"
> — George Eliot

You Don't Know How It Feels
by Susan Hobbs

Most parents don't know how it feels... and I hope you never do
To have a child that is special and to have all you're dreams taken from you

I had the same dreams; of ball games, driving, and first dates
Plans now have to change, at a very fast rate

Our lives now different: doctors, therapy, special schools, tests
It is hard and scary. I love my child, so I do my best

When I go out in public with him, just to have some fun
All the stares and comments, I just want to run

For some of us, we just cannot bare, all the tantrums and aggression
Some people think that we just don't care

The hardest decision in the world I had to make
Is the next one; to place him in a home
Please keep your opinion of my choice to yourself, for goodness sake

I take him to the home, that I have chosen to try
I leave him there, and all I can do is cry
I hope the workers will treat him as they should
My child cannot talk, please treat him good

I sit at home, he is on my mind - What is he thinking?
Does he wonder why I left him behind?
When I visit him, sometimes I see things that make me mad
I LOVE HIM so much! Don't treat him bad

I am not trying to be picky, I just want the best
He is a person, he deserves the best
and so do all the rest

I know when I complain
I make some people ill
Please don't take it out on him, if it were
your child how would you feel?

When I am at home
and I have to trust in what you do,
Please just think...
What if it wasn't him in that body,

...but you?

Photo by Susan Hobbs

145

About the Author

Judy Lynne was born and raised in Springfield, Virginia, a suburb of Washington, D.C. Her oldest daughter, Jill, who was born in 1984, was diagnosed with autism at the age of four and a half. Since that time Judy has worked hard to educate herself about autism so that she could best provide for Jill and be a strong advocate for her. In addition to working as a graphic designer and raising a child with autism, Judy served as the President of the Autism Society of Kansas in 1992. She taught  the Understanding Yourself and Others™ (UYO) course for Global Relationship Centers in Kansas City and for Starship Hope, a non-profit organization in St. Louis, Missouri.

In 2004, Judy wanted to combine her experience in raising a child with autism with her graphic design talent and decided to self-publish a book that she felt would help other mothers who were raising children with autism. That book, **Autism: Heartfelt Thoughts from Mothers**, was published in February 2005. Nearly 100 mothers, from all over the world, share their challenges, blessings, and words of wisdom in raising a child with autism, Aspergers and PDD. The book has served to let woman who have a child with autism know that they are not alone and has helped educate their friends and family members about what their life is really like.

Judy currently lives in Olathe, Kansas and does freelance work for *Flatpicking Guitar Magazine*. In addition to Jill, she has two other wonderful children, Brennan, age 16, and Marie, age 9 who are both kind, loving and protective of their sister.

Contact: Judy@AutismThoughts.com

To Jill
Who you are has brought so many together
You are my sunshine & I love you!
Always,
Mom